Kotlin Programming for Beginners

An Introduction to Learn the Kotlin Programming Language with Tutorials and Hands-On Examples

Table of Contents

1. Introduction

Kotlin is a cross-platform general purpose programming language. It is statically typed and supports multiple programming paradigms such as object oriented programming, functional programming, concurrent, etc. Kotlin is an open-source language released under *Apache License 2.0*. A Czech company called *JetBrains* (formerly known as *IntelliJ Software*) started working on the development of Kotlin programming language in the year 2011. The idea was to develop a new language to target the *Java Virtual Machine (JVM) platform*. As of 2020, the development costs of Kotlin language are borne by JetBrains and Kotlin trademark is protected by *Kotlin Foundation*. The name Kotlin comes from *Kotlin Island* near *St. Petersburg, Russia*.

In early 2012, initial version of Kotlin was made open source under *Apache 2* license. The first official version *Kotlin v1.0* was released in February 2016. In May 2017, Google announced first-class supportfor Kotlin, thus making it an official android application development language in addition to Java. Further, Google announced that Kotlin is the preferred android application development language in May 2019.

Kotlin is fully interoperable with Java. Kotlin compilers can target applications for *Java Virtual Machine (JVM)* and also build executable native code specific to a supported platform via **LLVM compiler toolchain**. Furthermore, Kotlin can also compile to JavaScript and build front-end for web applications.

1

Most of the professional software development using Kotlin happens using an *Integrated Development Environment (IDE)* although it is also possible to manually compile a Kotlin program using a command line based compiler. These development tools are available for Windows, Linux, MAC and FreeBSD. Target platforms include *macOS, Windows, Linux, FreeBSD, Android, iOS, WebAssembly, watchOS and tvOS*.

2. Scope

Being a general purpose programming language, Kotlin can be used to build different kind of software. You can develop desktop applications, web applications, mobile applications, etc. With Google making the preferred android app development language in 2019, a lot of Kotlin development that is happening today is geared towards android application development.

There are plenty of Kotlin libraries with which you can build machine learning applications, data science applications, REST APIs, etc. Something as simple as accessing databases like *MySQL, PostgreSQL, MongoDB, etc.* can be done using Kotlin with the help of the appropriate libraries. In fact, developing android applications can sometimes include heavy usage of *SQLite* which can easily be accomplished by this versatile programming language. Since Kotlin is fully interoperable with Java, all Java libraries can be imported in to your applications. Such multi-language software development is usually done using build automation tools such as *Gradle*.

Some of the famous android apps written in Kotlin are – *Pinterest, Uber, Coursera, Evernote, Kickstarter, etc.*

What are the prerequisites of learning Kotlin?

In order to learn Kotlin, you should be an adequately experienced user of a PC/Laptop. You should know your way around the system; know how to install/uninstall software; modify system properties; be comfortable with using the Command Prompt, Terminal, Shell, etc. -- understand how to navigate through directories, execute commands and so on. No prior knowledge of programming is needed. However, previous programming experience will definitely help. In fact, if you are a Java programmer, you will pick up Kotlin concepts really quickly and will also be able to migrate Java code to Kotlin if needed. Again, this book is written keeping in mind the absolute beginner. If you do not have any programming knowledge, you should still be able to learn Kotlin.

What will I learn from this book?

This book is intended for beginners who want to get started with Kotlin. I have tried to keep things as simple and as interesting as possible. This book will teach you the basics of Kotlin programming, how to compile and execute Kotlin programs and how to use IDE for Kotlin development.

Will this book teach me how to develop Android apps using Kotlin?

The short answer to this question is No! This book will teach you the basics of Kotlin and you will be able to develop simple console applications. These basic concepts are needed if you want to develop android apps or any other complex applications such as web services and web applications. Combining basic concepts and android development is beyond the scope of this book. However, you will also learn how professional level development takes place using Integrated Development Environment (IDE). With basic concepts and the knowledge of IDE, you will most likely be able to learn android application development on your own.

3. Getting Started

Kotlin compilers can target executable code for multiple platforms including Java Virtual Machine (JVM) and architecture specific native platforms. If you target for JVM, the compiler will generate *machine independent byte code* which will execute inside the JVM (*more on that later*) where as, when you target for a native platform, the compiler will generate an executable binary that will work only on that specific platform. There are pros and cons of both approaches. We will only learn how to target applications for the JVM. This approach is not just beginner friendly, it is also the widely used one. JVM is included in the Java environment and Kotlin compilers depend on Java Class Libraries which are a part of *Java Development Kit (JDK)*. All these requirements are included in *Java SE* distribution.

Note: If you use anything other than Windows, refer to the given links for OS specific installation.

3.1 Installing Java SE

Let us take a look at how to install Java on different operating systems.

3.1.1 Installing Java SE on Windows

This section will teach you how to set up Kotlin development tools on Windows. In order to install a software on Windows, you will need administrator rights. Make sure that you have administrator rights before proceeding.

Java SE is available for download free of cost from the *Oracle* website – https://www.oracle.com/java/technologies/javase-downloads.html. Visit the link and download the latest LTS version. You may need to create a free Oracle account if you do not have one. At the time of writing this book, the latest LTS version is *Java SE 11.*

Once you have the installation file, execute it to start the setup process. You will be greeted with a welcome screen like this:

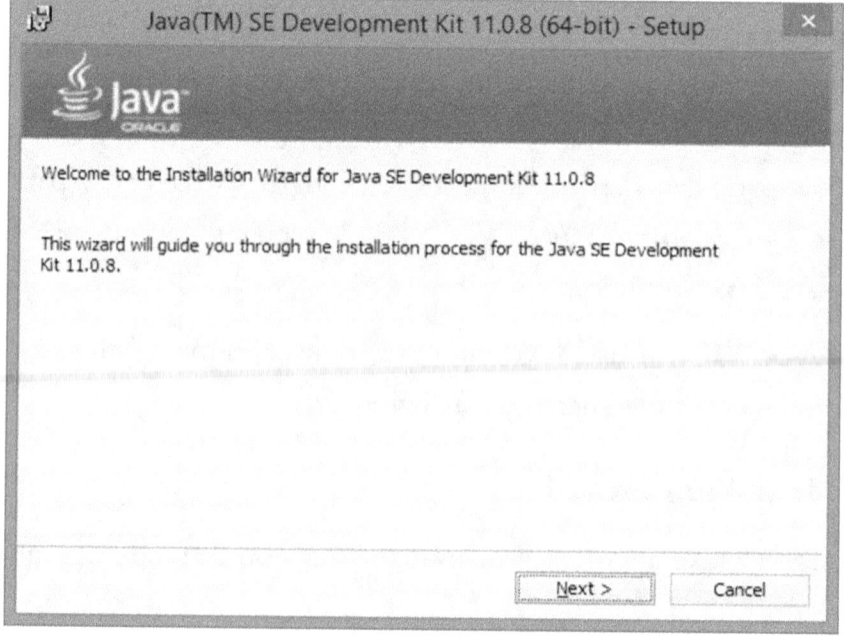

Click *Next.*

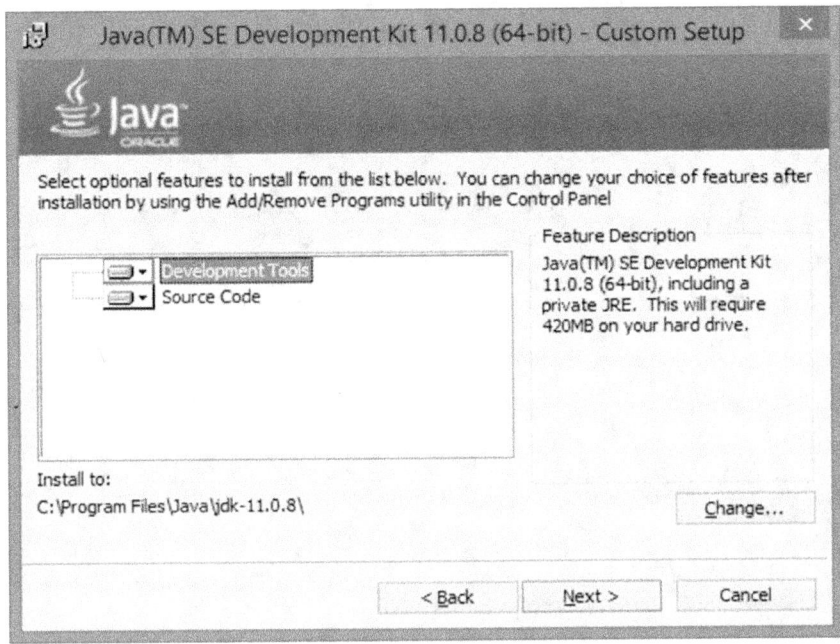

Here, you will be given options to customize the installation. It is best to leave these options unchanged; click *Next.*

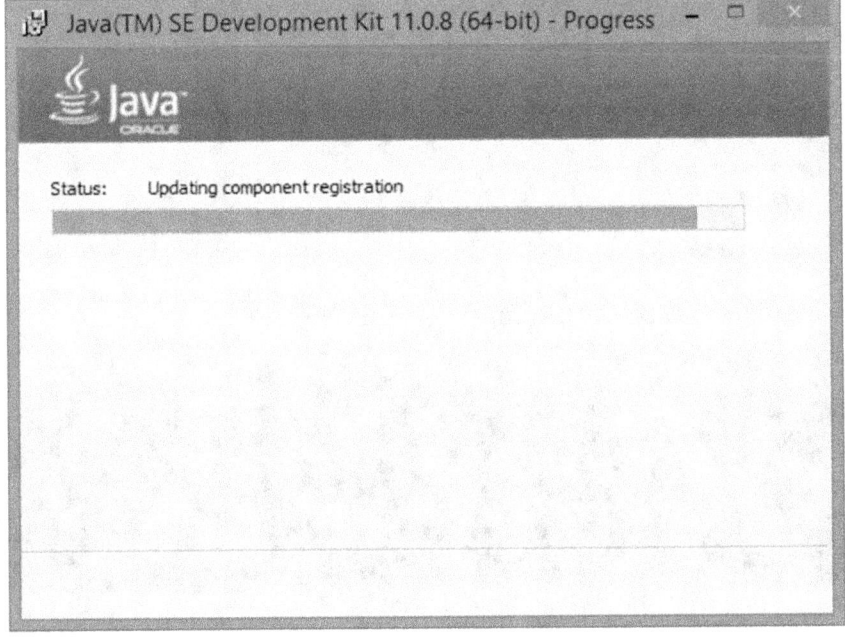

The setup process will not begin. This may take a few minutes to complete. Once done, you will see something like this:

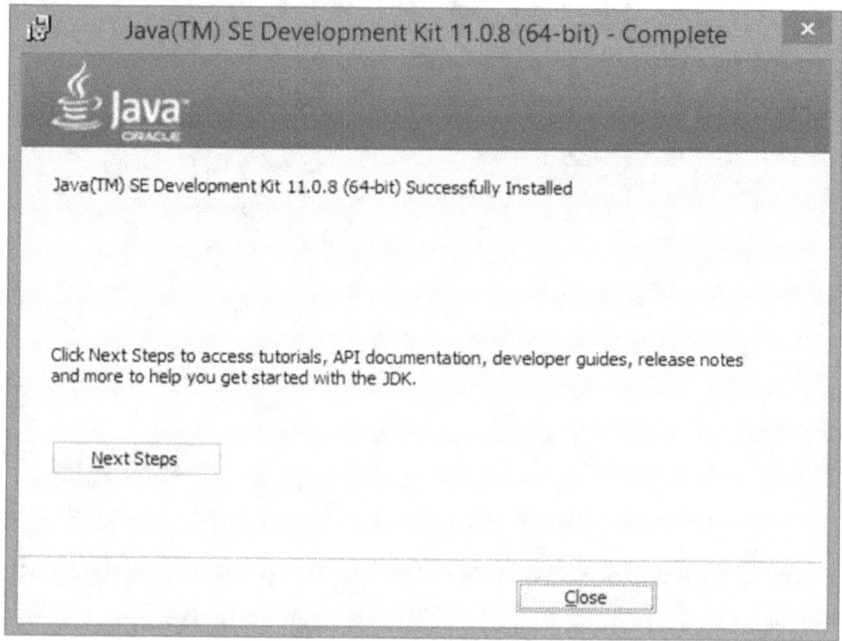

Click **Close** to exit the setup wizard.

You can check if Java SE has been installed correctly by opening the Command Prompt and entering the following commands:

java --version

javac --version

You should see something like this:

If you see an error here, for example – cannot find command or something similar, it means that there is a problem either with the installation or the environment variables are not set properly. In such a case, go through the installation process again.

3.1.2 Installing Java SE on Unix based OS

If you are using a Unix based OS such as Linux, macOS, FreeBSD, DragonflyBSD, etc., it is most likely that Java SE came pre-installed with the OS distribution. In order to check if Java is present, enter the following commands one by one in the Shell/ Terminal:

$>java -version

$>javac -version

If Java is present on the system, the above commands will return the versions as follows:

If the terminal returns command not found error, it means Java is not present. In such a case, you will have to download the appropriate installation file from https://www.oracle.com/java/ technologies/javase-downloads.html and follow the installation process specific to your OS.

3.2 Setup Command Line Kotlin Compiler

A compiler is a software that compiles a program into executable code. Kotlin Compiler is maintained by JetBrains on GitHub. Regardless of which operating system you use, visit this link – https://github.com/JetBrains/kotlin/releases/ to download the latest stable version of the compiler – *kotlin-compiler-<version>.zip*. <u>Do not download</u> *kotlin-native-windows-<version>.zip* as the native version is used to target applications for the native platform and not JVM. At the time of writing this book, the latest version is *kotlin-compiler-1.4.10* available at https://github.com/JetBrains/kotlin/releases/tag/v1.4.10. Once you have the file, unpack the archive to a convenient location. Navigate to the directory where the archive has been extracted and locate the *bin* folder. For example, if you have extracted the archive to this location – *C:\Kotlin\kotlinc*, the path to the bin folder should be *C:\Kotlin\kotlinc\bin*. This is very important because the *bin* folder contains all the scripts needed to compile Kotlin programs on different operating systems. On Unix based systems, if you have extracted the archive to say */home/<user>/kotlinc*, the bin directory will be located at */home/<user>/kotlinc/bin*.

3.2.1 Setup Kotlin Compiler on Windows

Once you have extracted the downloaded archive, next step is to add path to the bin folder to the *Environment Variable* called *Path*. This will make sure that the Kotlin compiler can be accessed from anywhere inside the Command Prompt regardless of the working directory. To do so, open *System Properties*, click on *Advanced* tab and click on *Environment Variables*:

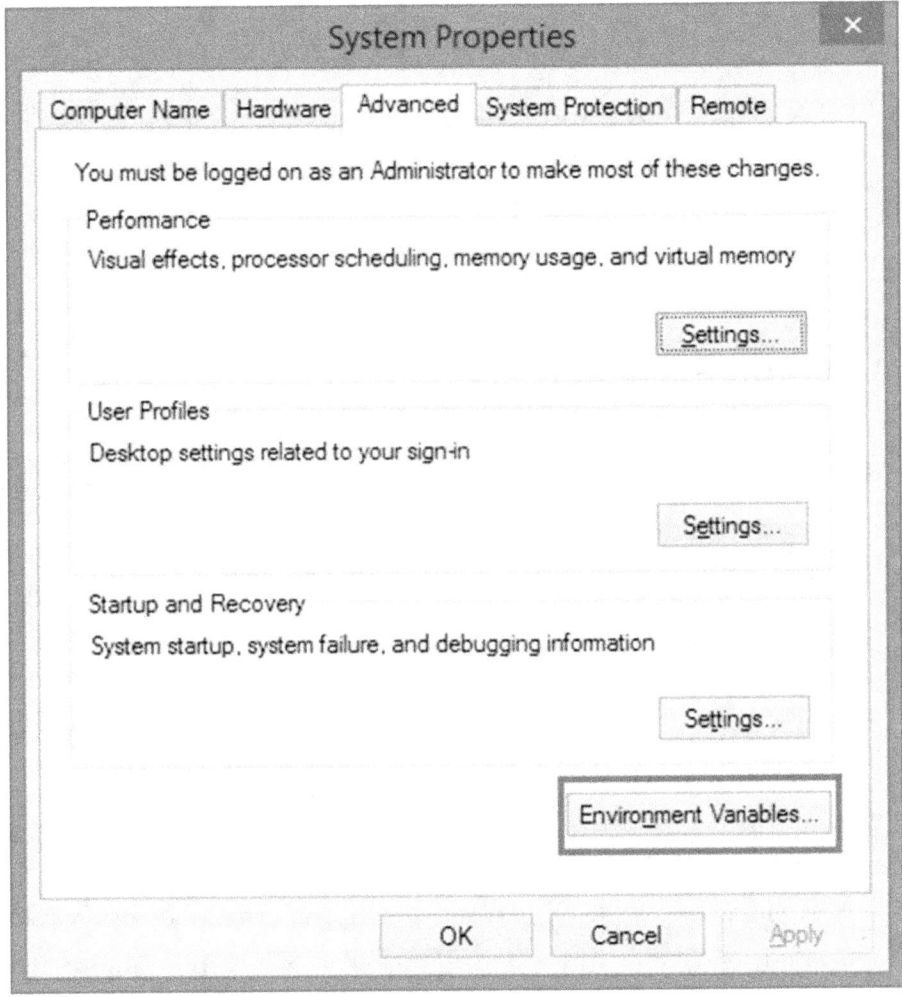

In the new window that opens, under *System variables*, select *Path* and click *Edit.*

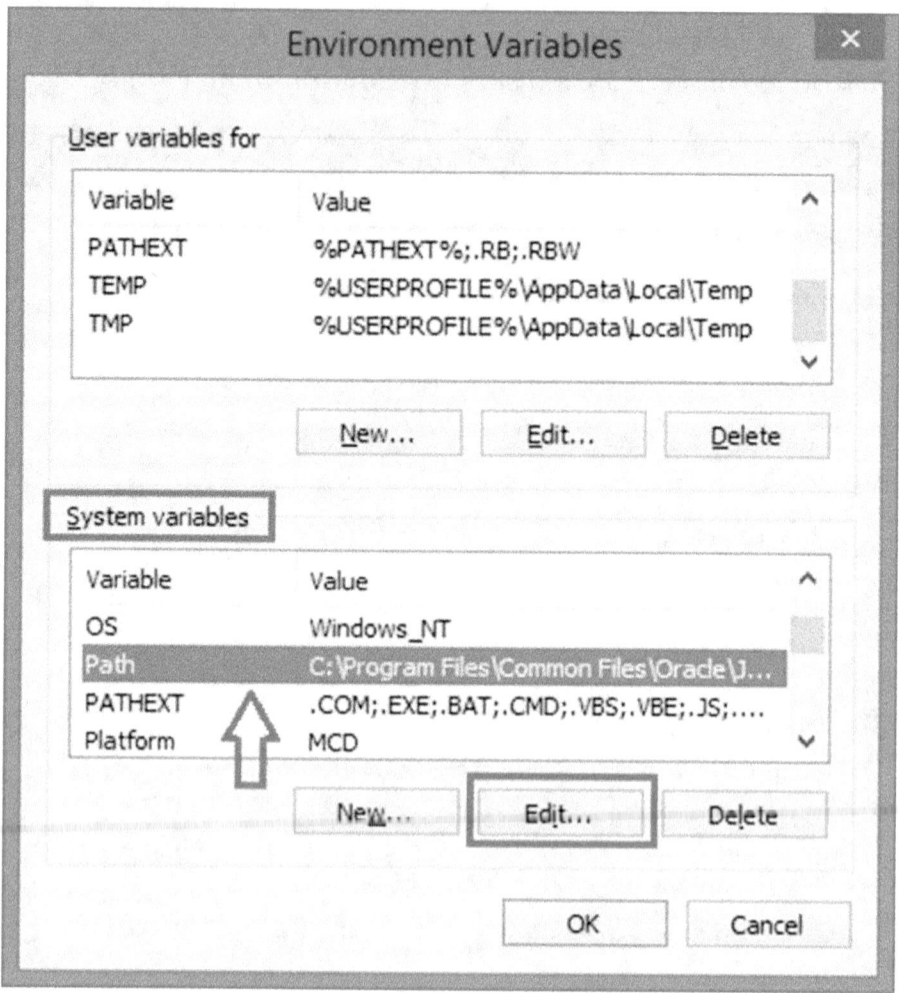

A small window will open which will have the current value of the Path variable. Add a semi-colon to the existing contents of the variable value if it is not present, append path to bin directory and click OK.

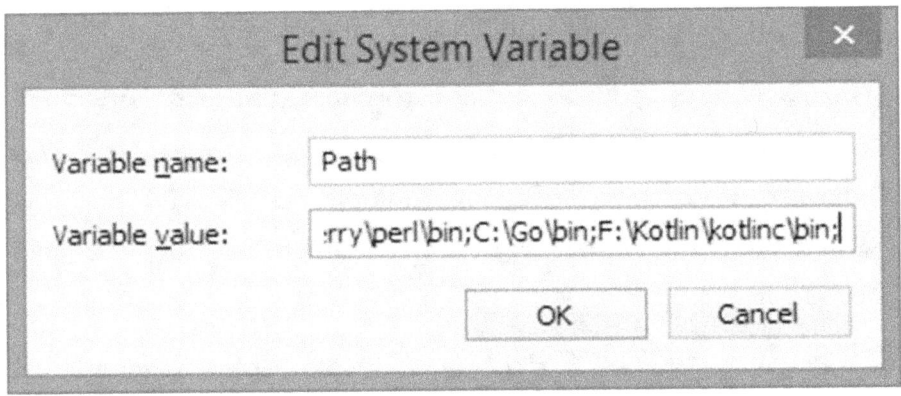

Close all other windows related to system properties. Open Command Prompt and enter the following command:

kotlinc -version

You should see something like this:

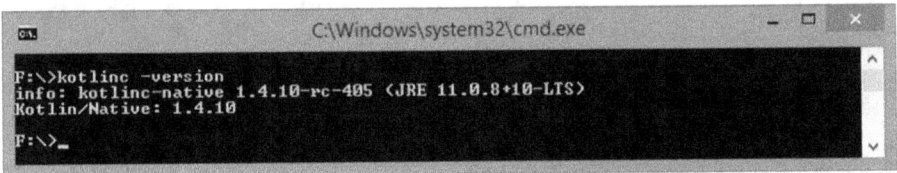

If you see an error which looks something like – " *'kotlinc' is not recognized as an internal or external command, operable program or batch file.* ", it means that the *Path* variable has not been set properly to point to the *bin* directory of the Kotlin compiler. In such a case, unpack the compiler's archive once again (download it again if necessary) to an easily accessible location, locate the *bin* folder after unpacking and follow the process of adding path to bin directory to the *Path Environment Variable.*

3.2.2 Setup Kotlin Compiler on Unix based OS

Determine the path to *bin* directory inside the directory where you have unpacked the compiler's archive and add it to the *PATH* environment variable. There are multiple ways to do this. For example, you can use the *export* command inside the Terminal/ Shell as follows:

$>export PATH="${PATH}:<path to Kotlin compiler's bin directory>"

Example:

$>export PATH="${PATH}:/home/user123/compilers/kotlinc/bin"

Note: This method will make new additions to the PATH variable volatile in nature. That is, path to bin directory will be available in the current session only. Once you close that terminal and open again, this addition will already have vanished. You may check the contents of the PATH variable using the *echo* command as follows:

$>echo $PATH

Alternatively, in most Unix based distributions, you can append the *export* command shown above to *~/.bashrc* file at the bottom. This file is a shell script that executes every time a terminal is launched. As a result, your *export* command will be executed every time you open a terminal and thus you will have the desired value of the PATH variable. Once all this is set up, execute the following command:

$>kotlinc -version

You should see something like this:

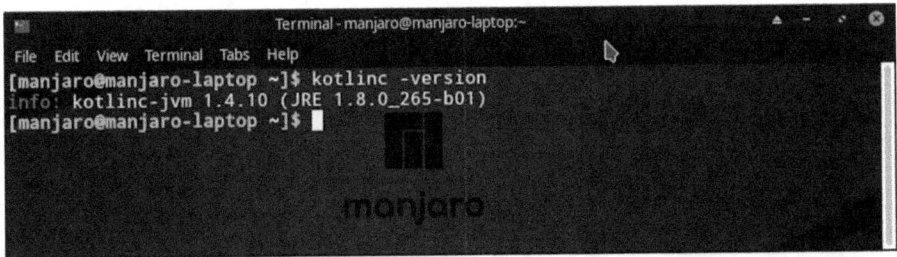

If you see the command not found error, it can mean one of two things – either the compiler's archive has not been extracted properly or the PATH variable has not been set to point to the bin directory. Use **echo $PATH** command to check contents of the PATH variable and take necessary action.

3.3 Setup Integrated Development Environment (IDE)

An integrated development environment is a software that provides a set of tools and facilities to a programmer for software development. In this section, we will learn how to set up two different IDEs for Kotlin development. The installation will be demonstrated only for Windows as the installation process will vary from OS to OS. Once you have installed the desired IDE installed, the setup process shall be more or less the same.

3.3.1 IntelliJ IDEA

IntelliJ IDEA is an IDE by JetBrains (the same company behind Kotlin development). The IDE supports several JVM languages including Kotlin. The community edition is available free of cost at this link – https://www.jetbrains.com/idea/download/. Download the appropriate setup file for your operating systems. This section contains the setup process of IntelliJ IDEA on Windows.

Once you have the setup file, execute it. You will be greeted with a welcome scree that looks something like this:

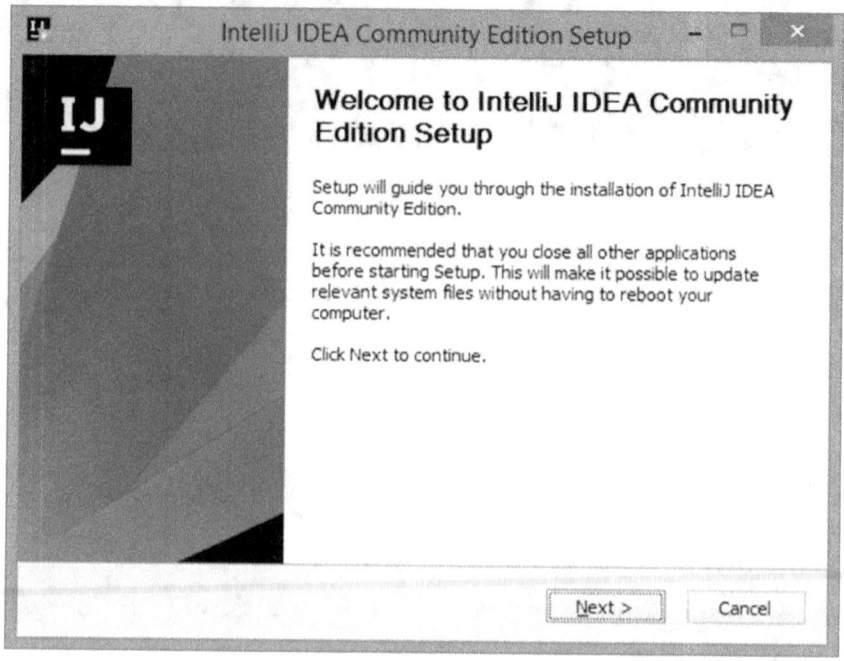

Click **Next** and the setup process will continue.

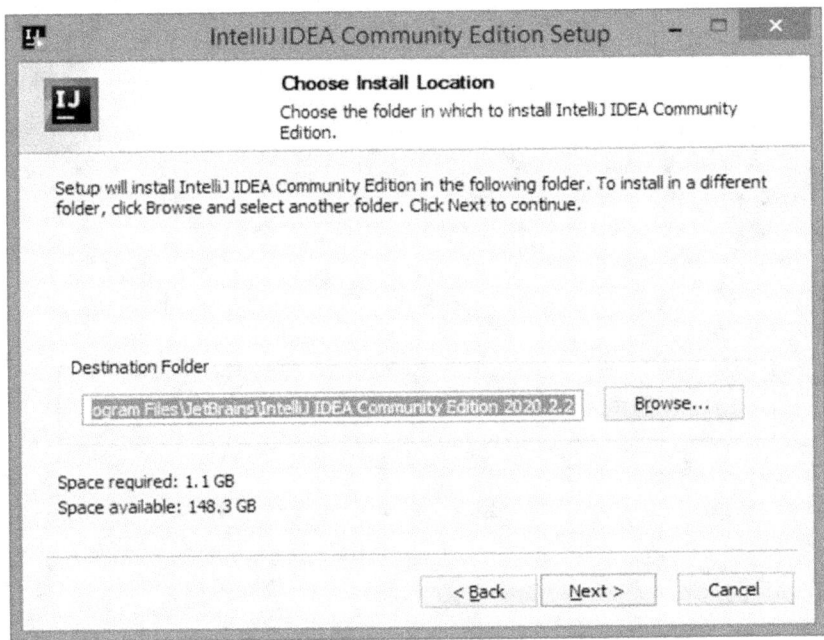

Here, you can set the directory where this IDE will be installed. It is best to leave this unchanged. Click *Next*.

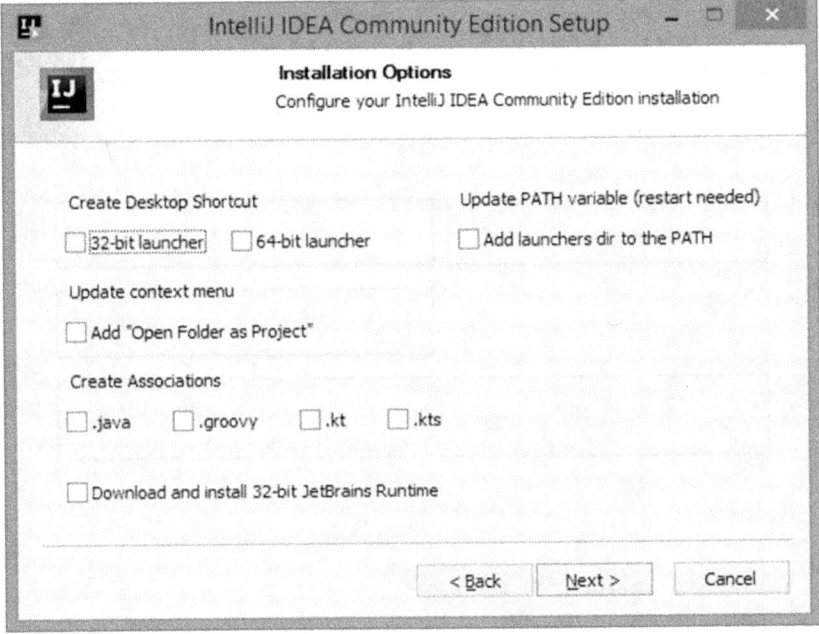

Here, you will be given an option to customize installation. It is best to leave these options as they are and click *Next.*

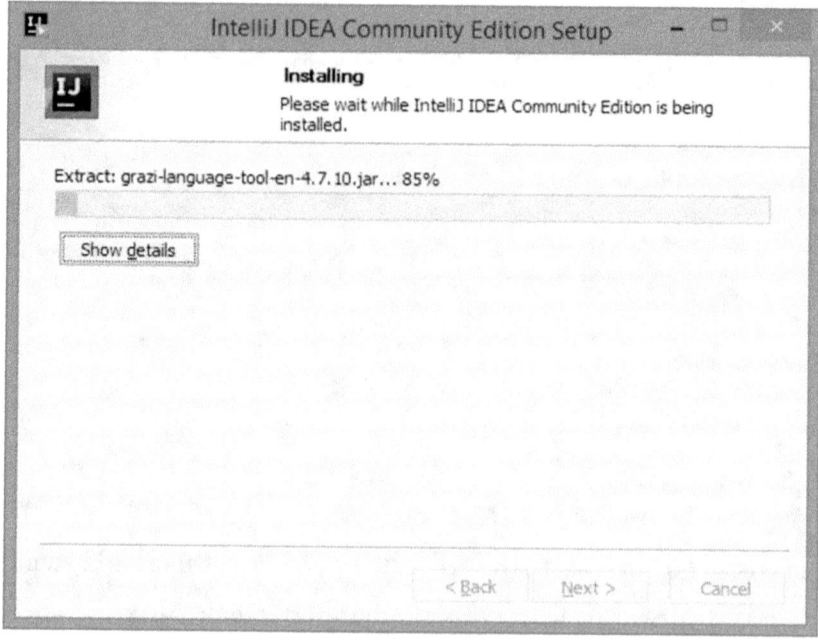

The setup process will now begin and may take a few minutes to complete.

Once the setup process is over, you will see something like this:

Depending on your installation options, you may need to reboot your system. Once everything is done, run the *IntelliJ IDEA* application.

During the first run, you may be presented with the privacy policy or an agreement:

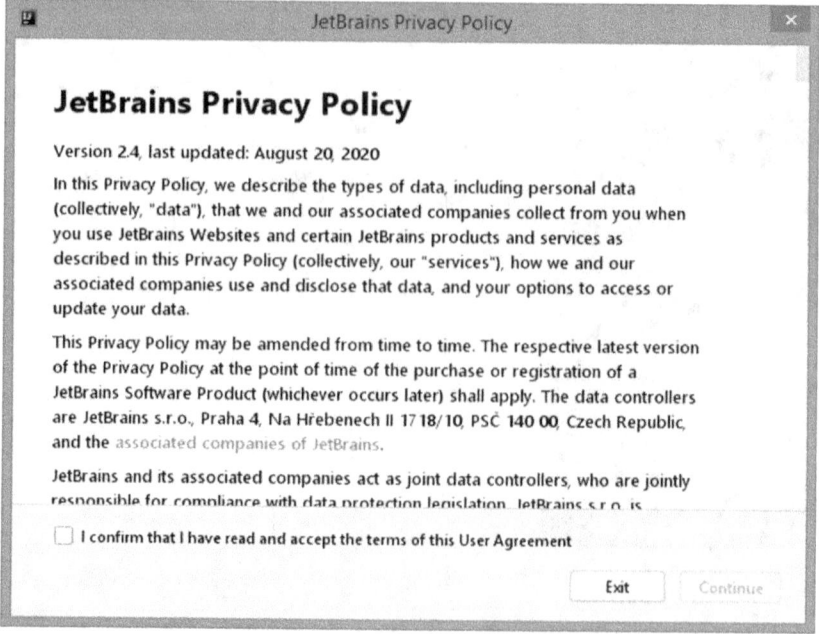

Read the agreement, accept the terms and click *Continue*.

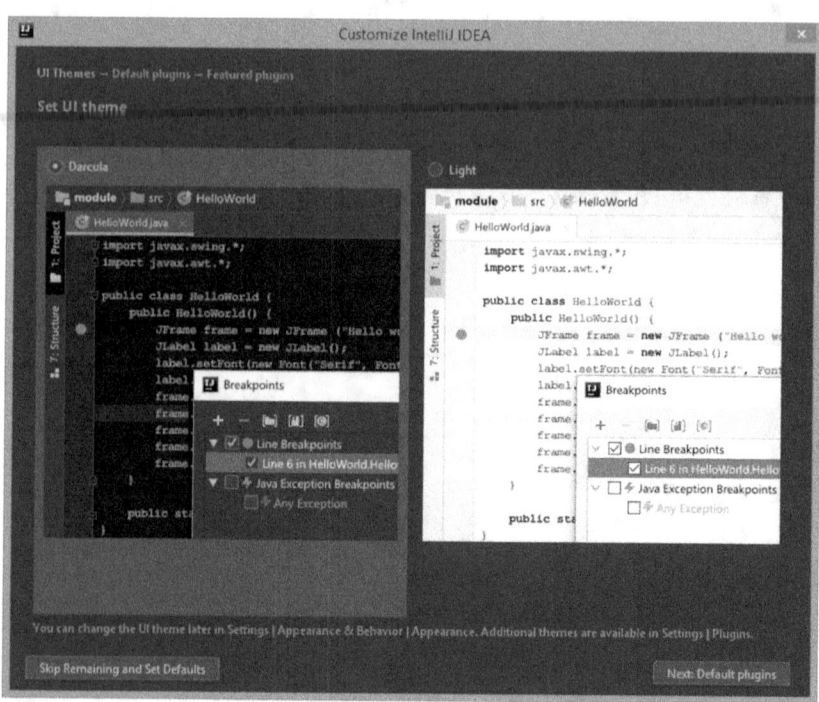

This is where you will be given options to customize the IDE. It is best to skip this step.

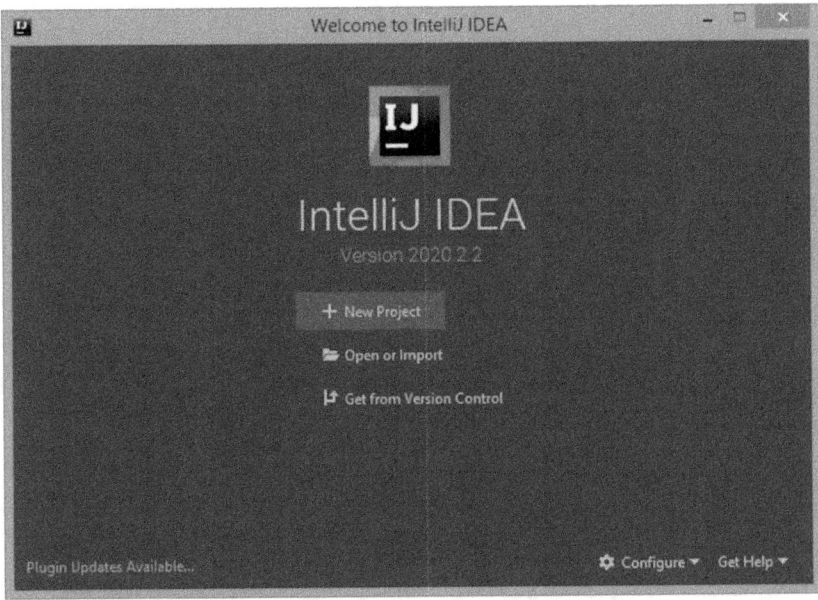

This is what you will see once everything is done. It is from this place that you can start a new project or open an existing one.

3.3.2 Eclipse IDE

Eclipse is a popular IDE, very famous among Java developers but supports many more languages such as C, C++, Python, etc. Kotlin development can be done inside Eclipse using the official Kotlin plug-in. Eclipse can be downloaded from this link – https://www.eclipse.org/downloads/. Download the appropriate setup file for your operating system. This section will demonstrate how to setup Eclipse on Windows.

Run the setup file once you have downloaded it. You see a welcome screen like this:

eclipse installer by Oomph

type filter text   Q

Eclipse IDE for Java Developers

The essential tools for any Java developer, including a Java IDE, a Git client, XML Editor, Maven and Gradle integration

Eclipse IDE for Enterprise Java Developers

Tools for developers working with Java and Web applications, including a Java IDE, tools for Web Services, JPA and Data Tools, JavaServer Pages and Faces, Mylyn,...

Eclipse IDE for C/C++ Developers

An IDE for C/C++ developers.

Eclipse IDE for Web and JavaScript Developers

The essential tools for any JavaScript developer, including JavaScript, TypeScript, HTML, CSS, XML, Yaml, Markdown... languages support; Kubernetes, Angular and...

Eclipse IDE for PHP Developers

The essential tools for any PHP developer, including PHP language support, Git client, Mylyn and editors for JavaScript, TypeScript, HTML, CSS and XML.
Click here to...

Click on *Eclipse IDE for Java Developers.*

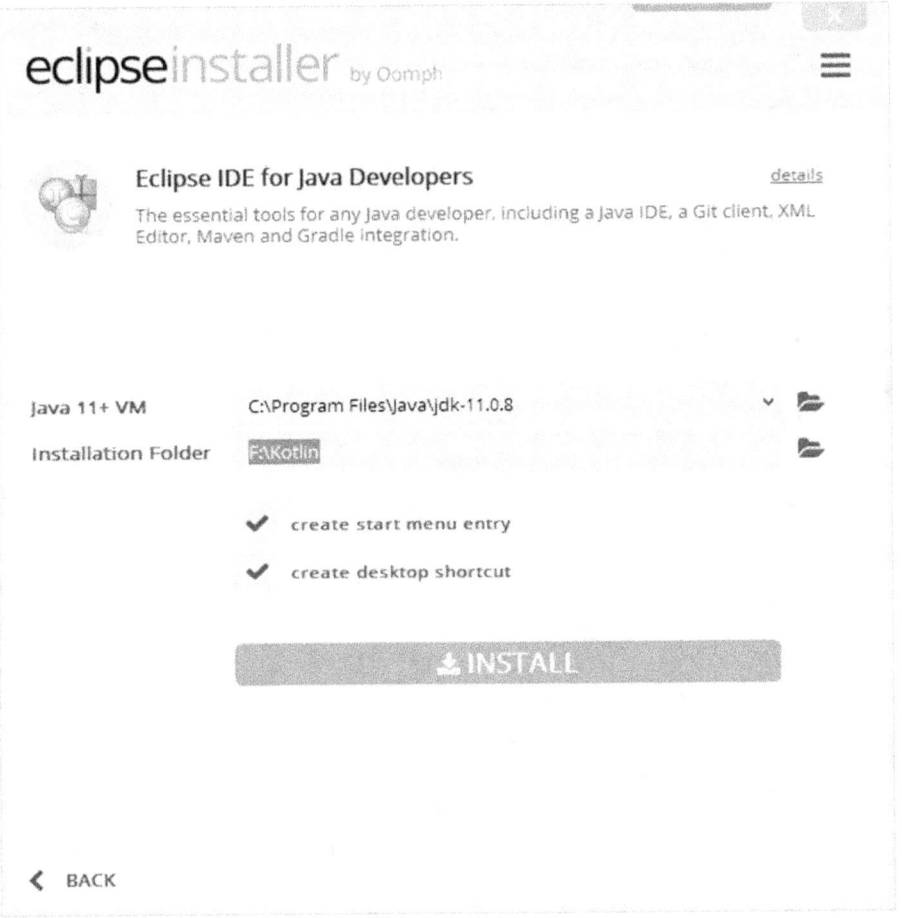

The setup process will automatically detect the Java version installed on your system. Further, you may chose the directory where Eclipse is to be installed or leave it as it is. Click *Install* to continue.

You will be presented with a user agreement. Read the terms and click *Accept Now.*

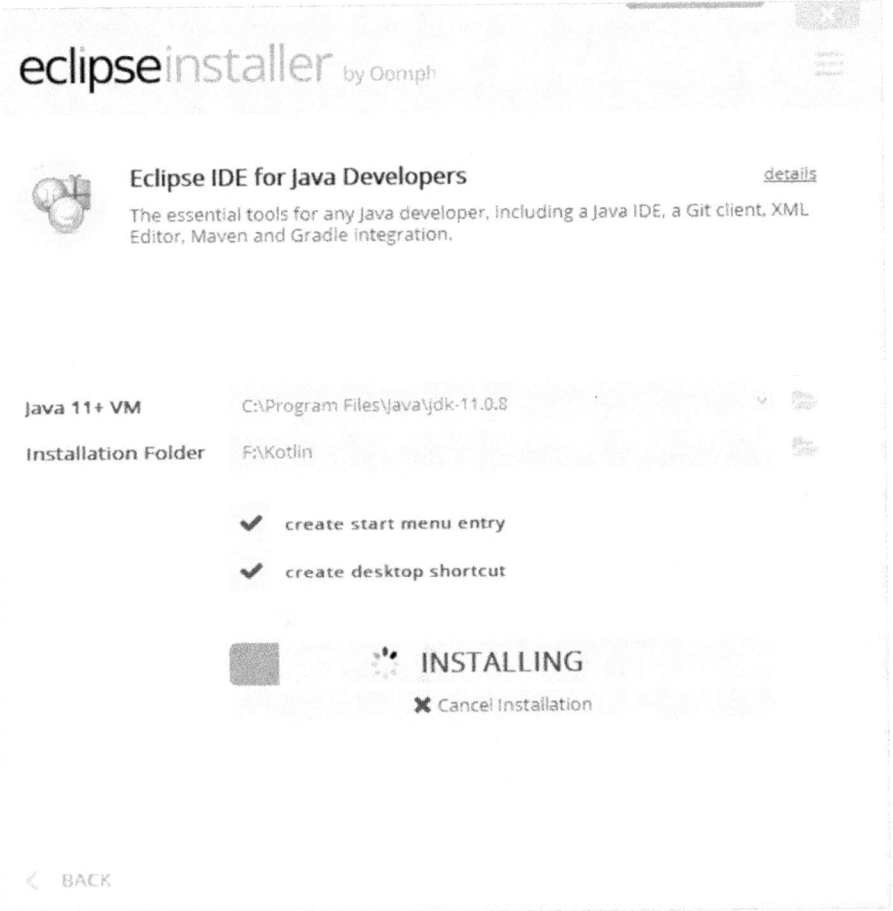

The installation process will now begin and may take a few minutes to complete.

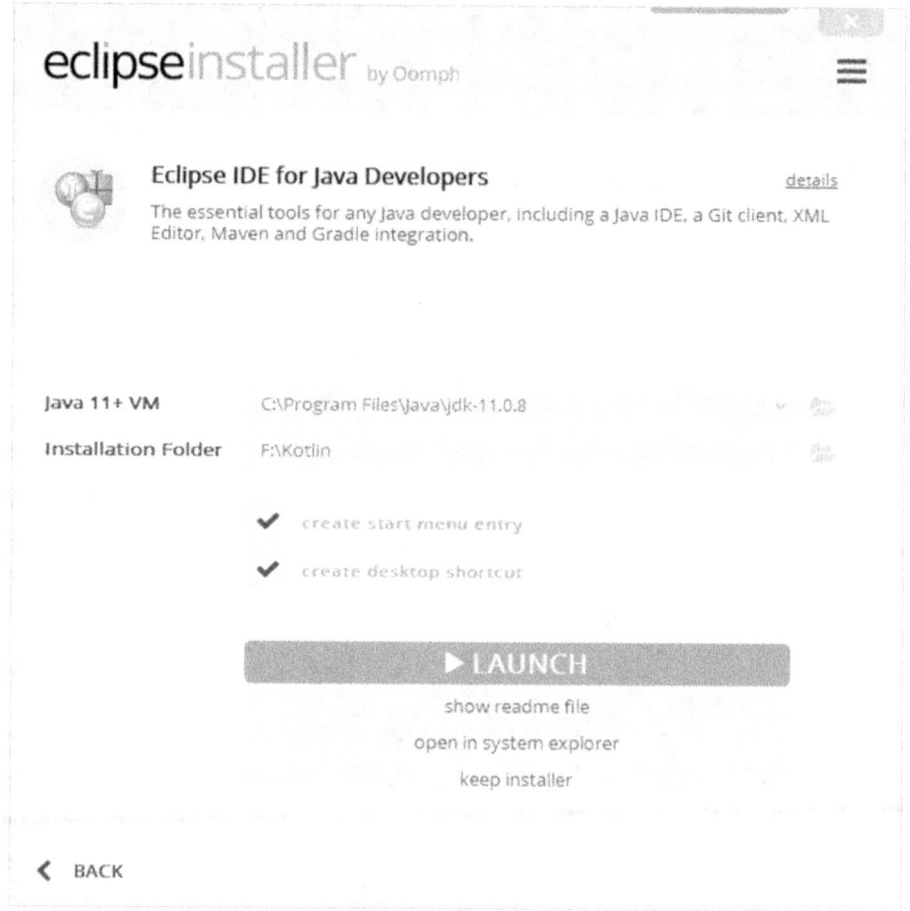

You will see something like this once the installation process is over. Click *LAUNCH* to start Eclipse IDE.

You will be asked to select a workspace directory where all your projects will be saved. This can be changed later on.

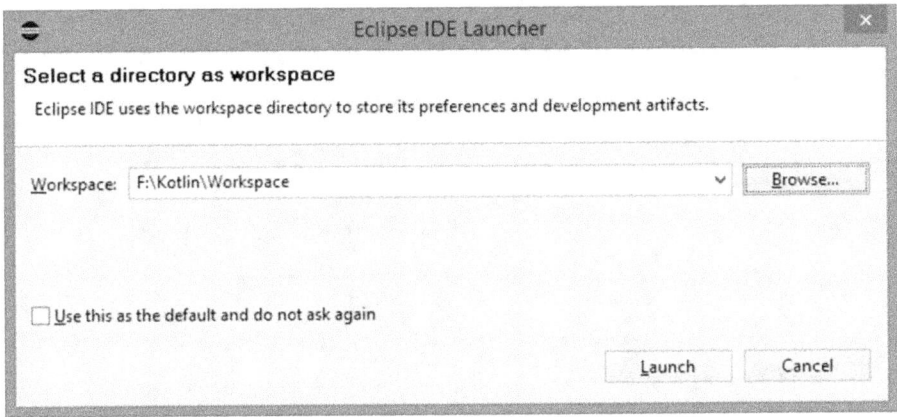

Click **Launch** when ready.

This is how the Eclipse IDE's main Window looks like:

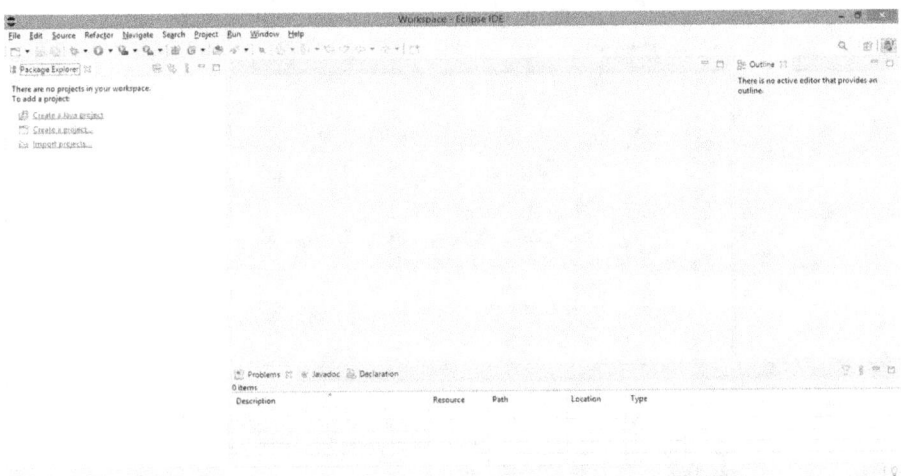

This IDE is good for Java development. For Kotlin development, a Kotlin plug-in is needed. To install this plug-in, click *Help -> Marketplace*.

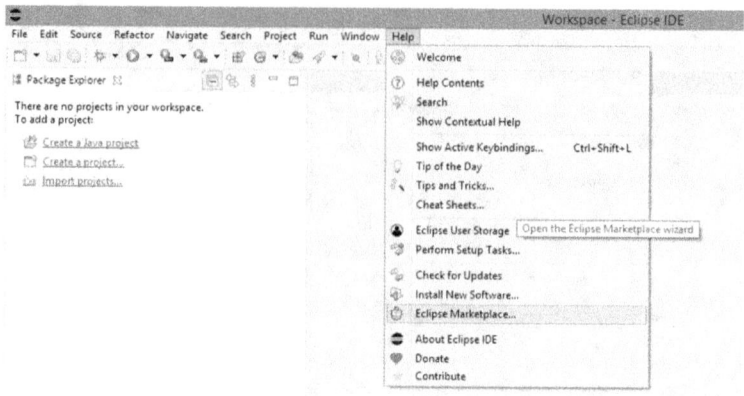

A Window will open from where you can install various plugins. Type Kotlin in the search box and press Enter:

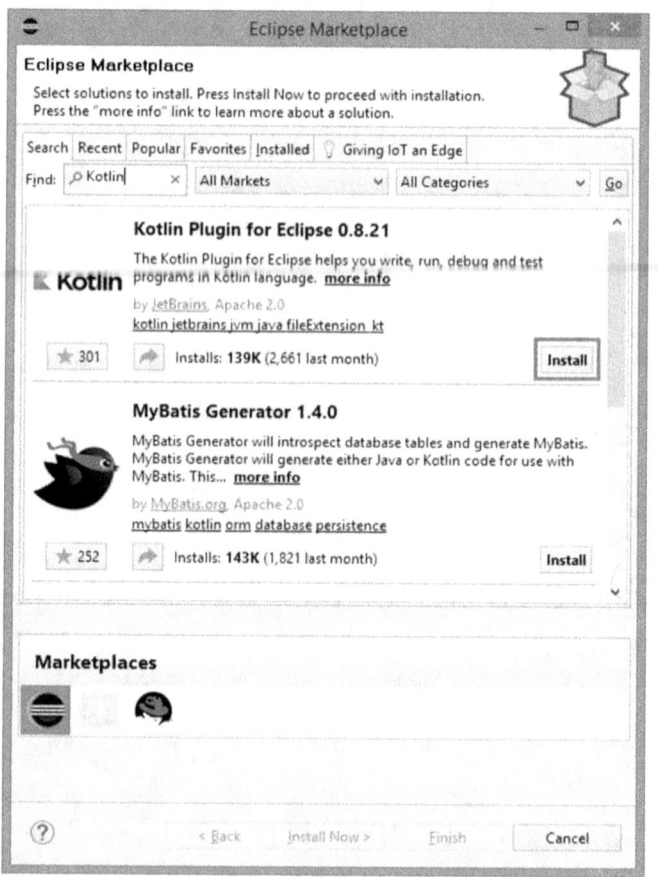

Click *Install* to install the Kotlin Plug-in for Eclipse.

You will be presented with a licence agreement:

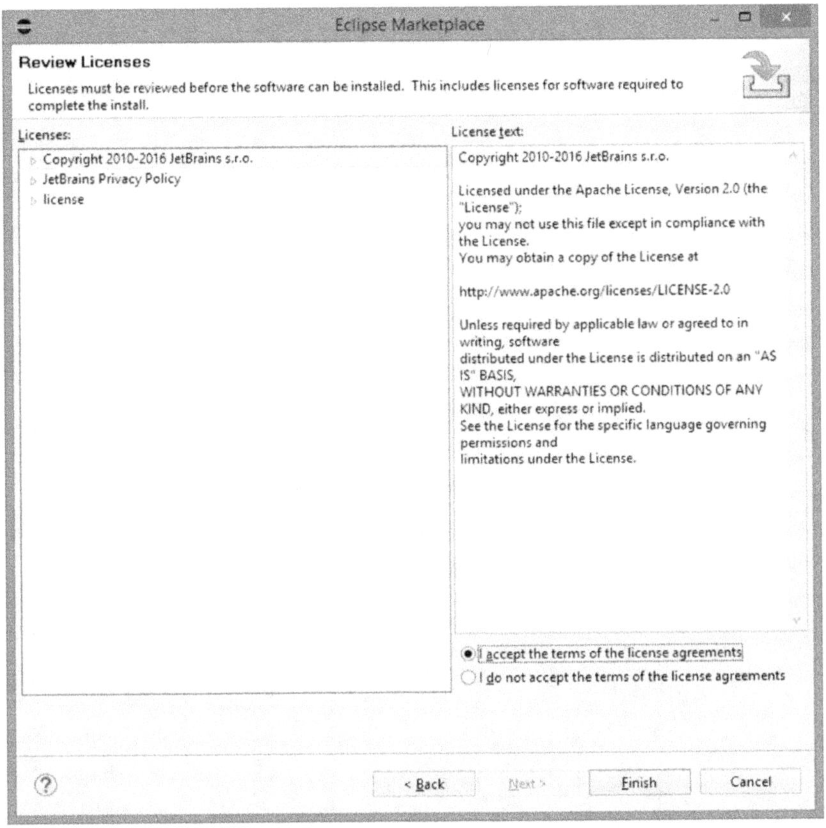

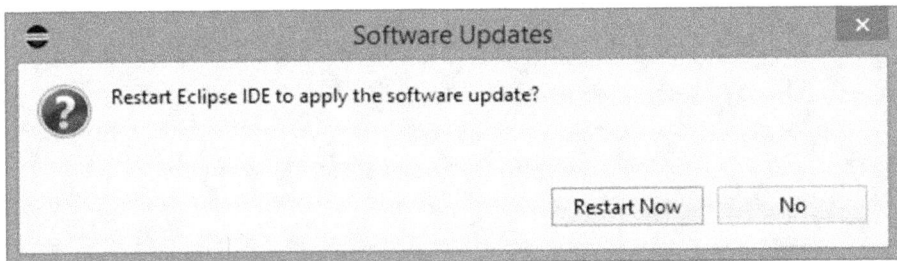

Read the agreement, accept the terms and click *Finish*.

Once the plug-in is installed, you will be asked to restart the IDE. Click *Restart Now*.

4. Building Kotlin Applications

In this book, all the applications that we are going to build will be targeted for the *Java Virtual Machine (JVM)*. This concept is very important. Our applications will not be native to a particular platform but will run inside JVM. Before learning how to build Kotlin applications, let us take a quick look at how applications are built in general.

An application contains a set of executable instructions that a computer understands. A native application has instructions that are specific to a particular platform. Normally, a program (or a group of programs) is written which defines what the target application should do. This program is given to a compiler which converts it into an executable binary; this is what we call as an application. Consider the following conceptual block diagram.

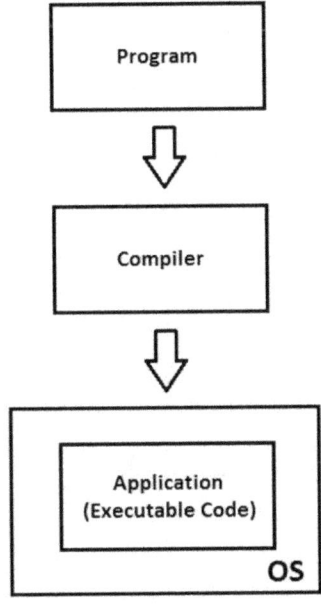

The actual compilation goes well beyond a three stage process but the above diagram is accurate at a conceptual level. A program is compiled by the compiler to generate executable code. If the executable code is native to a particular platform, it will run only on that platform. For example, native code meant for an x86 platform will not run on ARM platform; native application meant for Windows will not run on Linux and so on. Applications that are targeted for the JVM follow a slightly different approach. Let us first understand what is Java Virtual Machine in brief – JVM is a virtual machine that can execute Java bytecode. This bytecode is machine-independent. Primarily, JVM is used to run applications written in Java but can also run applications written in other languages such as Scala, Groovy, Kotlin, etc. A compiler that targets applications for the JVM generates Java bytecode that the JVM understands. Tomorrow, if a new programming language called XYZ is developed and its compiler ABC can generate Java bytecode, applications written in XYZ can run inside the Java Virtual Machine. Take a look at the following conceptual block diagram of how a JVM application is compiled and run:

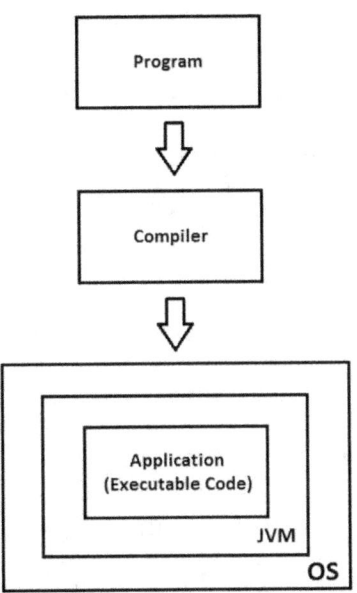

4.1 Kotlin Compiler

A Kotlin program is a plain-text file that can be written in any text editor such as Notepad, Wordpad, Notepad++, etc. Kotlin program files carry the extension *.kt*. The Kotlin compiler can compile a Kotlin program to Java bytecode that can run inside JVM. Normally, Java bytecode files carry the extension *.class*. Multiple *.class* files can be packaged into a single file called Java Archive which has the extension *.jar*. Such files are informally called JAR files. A JVM can execute *.class* files as well as *.jar* files. You do not have to worry about this intermediate process as the Kotlin compiler directly generates *.jar* files.

The general syntax of using the Kotlin compiler to build JAR files by compiling Kotlin programs is:

kotlinc <Kotlin Program> -include-runtime -d <Output file.jar>

Example:

kotlinc program1.kt -include-runtime -d program1.jar

The above command will build the executable JAR file for you but will not execute on its own. The JAR file can be executed using the following command:

java -jar <JAR file>

Example:

java -jar program1.jar

Let us see how to write a Kotlin program, compile it to a JAR file and then execute it. Open your favourite text editor, copy-paste the following code and save it as **test.kt** at a convenient location:

```kotlin
fun main() {
println("\nThis is a test program. If you see this,
you are doing great so far!!!\n")

}
```

Note: The above Kotlin program prints some text on the console. You need not understand the code now. The following chapters in this book will teach you concepts with which you will learn to write your own Kotlin programs. In this chapter, all you have to learn is how to compile and execute a Kotlin program.

Open **Command Prompt** or **Powershell** on **Windows** or **Terminal/Shell** on **Linux/macOS/FreeBSD**, navigate to the directory where you have saved **test.kt** and enter the following command:

kotlinc test.kt -include-runtime -d test.jar

The above command will invoke the Kotlin compiler, compile **test.kt** and build **test.jar**. The JAR file can be run using the following command:

java -jar test.jar

Here is what the result will look like on Windows:

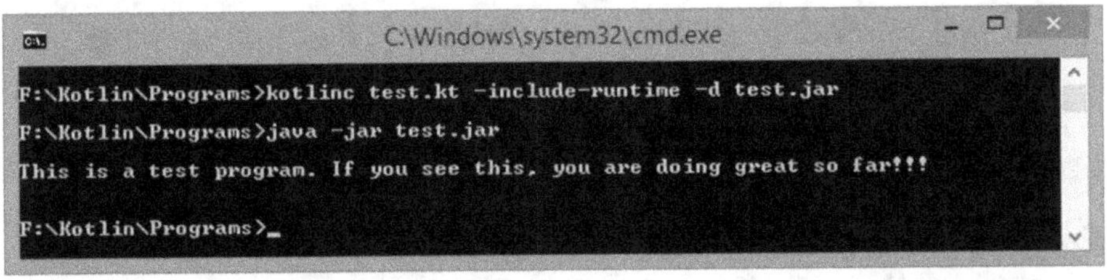

You will see the same result on a Unix-like OS. It looks like this on Linux:

4.2 IntelliJ IDEA

Run IntelliJ IDEA application on your system, a window that looks similar to the one shown below shall launch:

Click *New Project.*

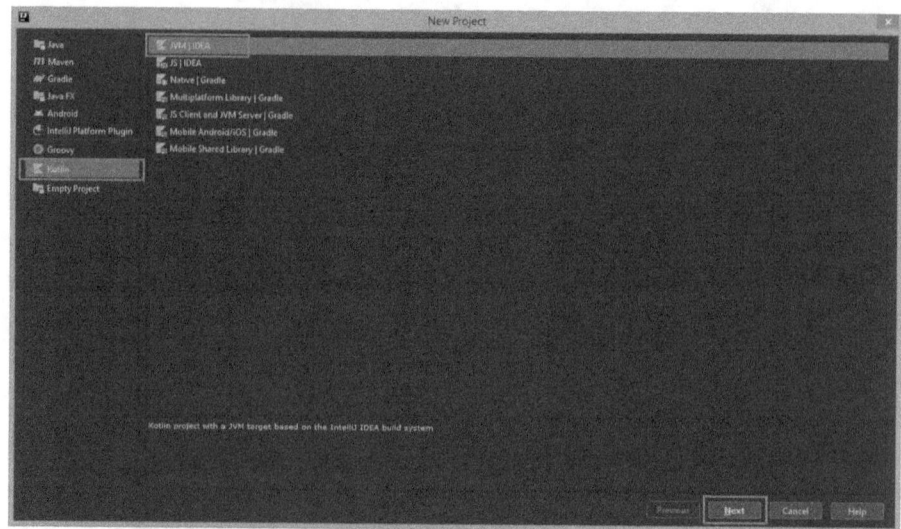

Select *Kotlin* from the left box and *JVM / IDEA* in the right box as shown in the image above. Click *Next* when done.

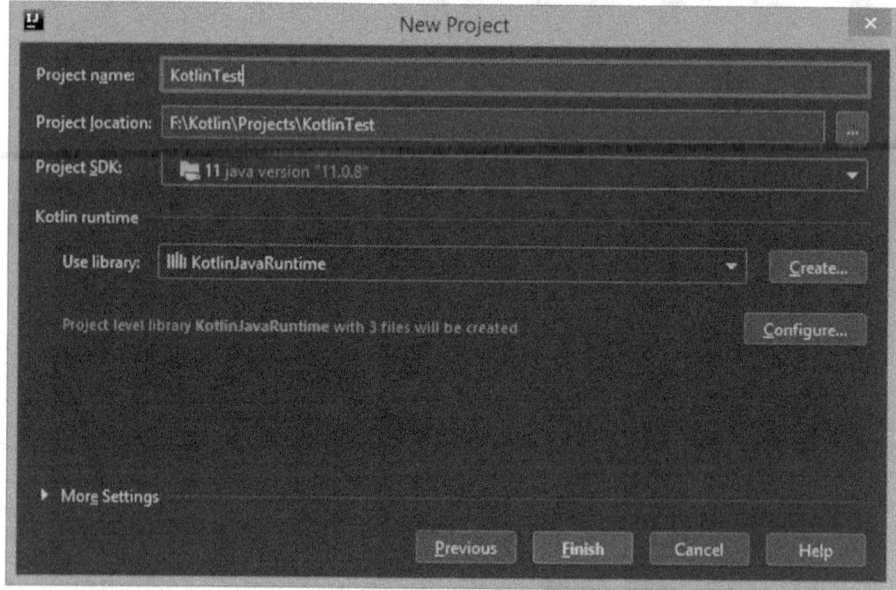

Give your project a name, select the location and click *Finish*.

The IDE will set up the project. On the left hand side, there will be a *Project* tool window. If it is not there, you can restore it from *View -> Tool Windows -> Project* menu. When a project is created, the IDE will create a new directory in its name. That directory will have all the necessary files and directories needed for the project to run correctly. The project that you just created and all the files and resources belonging to this project will be listed in this window. Expand your project's tree and you should see an *src* folder. In the programming world, *src* is short for source. Programs can alternatively be called source or source code.

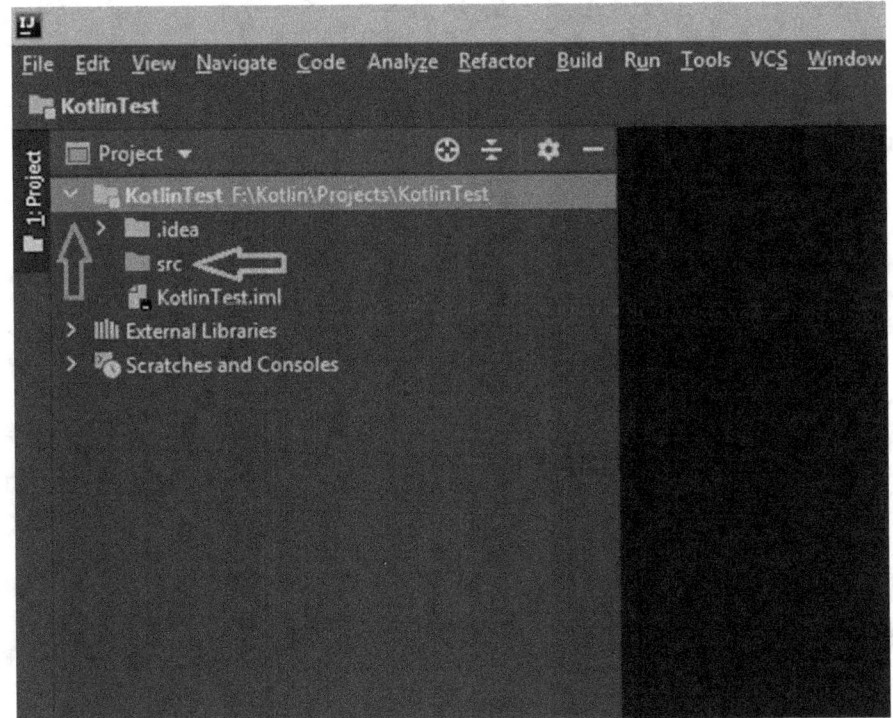

You will be placing Kotlin programs under the *src* folder. To do so, right-click on the folder and select *New -> Kotlin File/Class*.

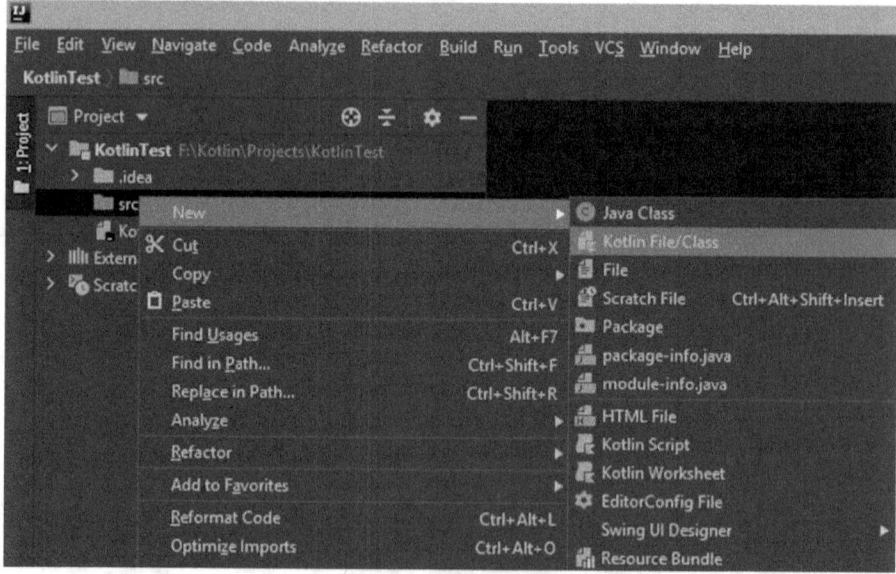

A small box will open where you will be able to enter the name of the source file:

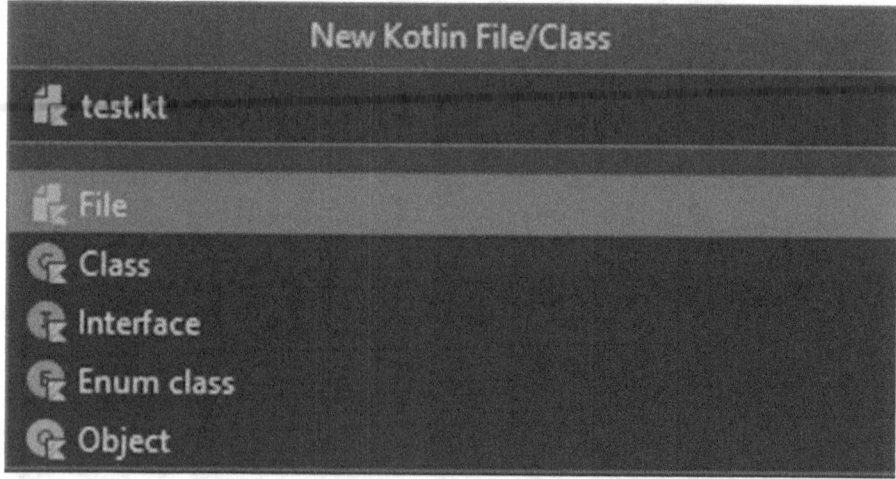

Enter the file name, select *File* and press *Enter.*

A text editor will launch within the IDE from where you can edit this newly created Kotlin program file (***test.kt***). At any point, you can double-click on the source file under *Project* to launch the built-in text editor.

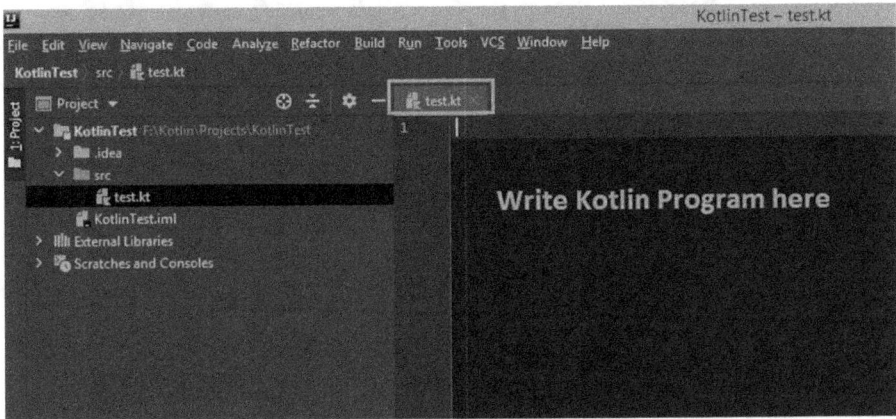

Copy-paste the Kotlin program from *Section 4.1* into the editor and save the file. Once there is runnable code inside a source file, a small green coloured Run/Play button will appear near the first line of code:

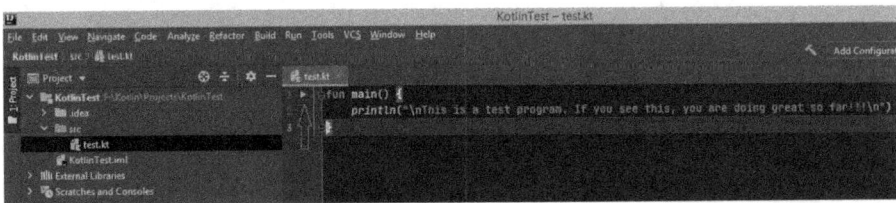

Click that button and then click *Run* to build this application and run it. Alternatively, you can do this by clicking *Run -> Run* from the menu bar. You will see the output in a window placed at the bottom half of the screen:

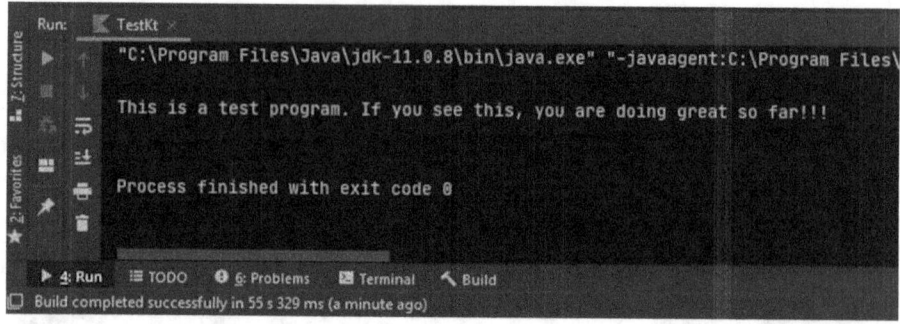

4.3 Eclipse IDE

Launch the Eclipse application on your system. The main window will look somewhat like this:

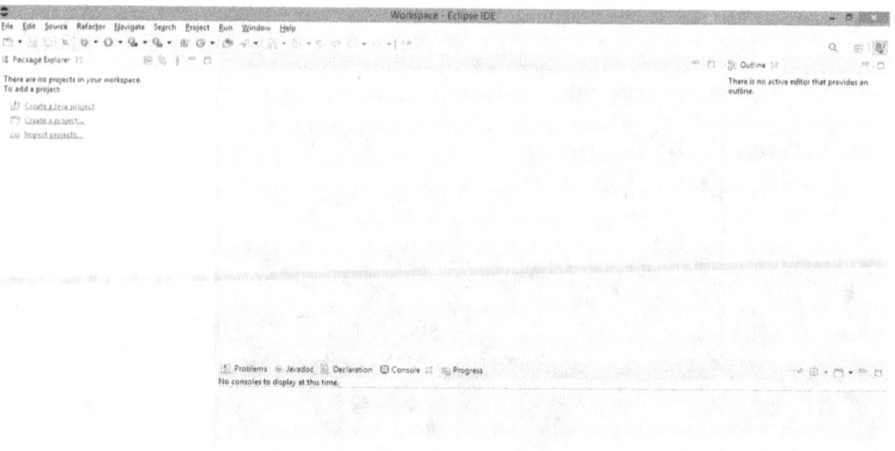

Click *File -> New -> Project.*

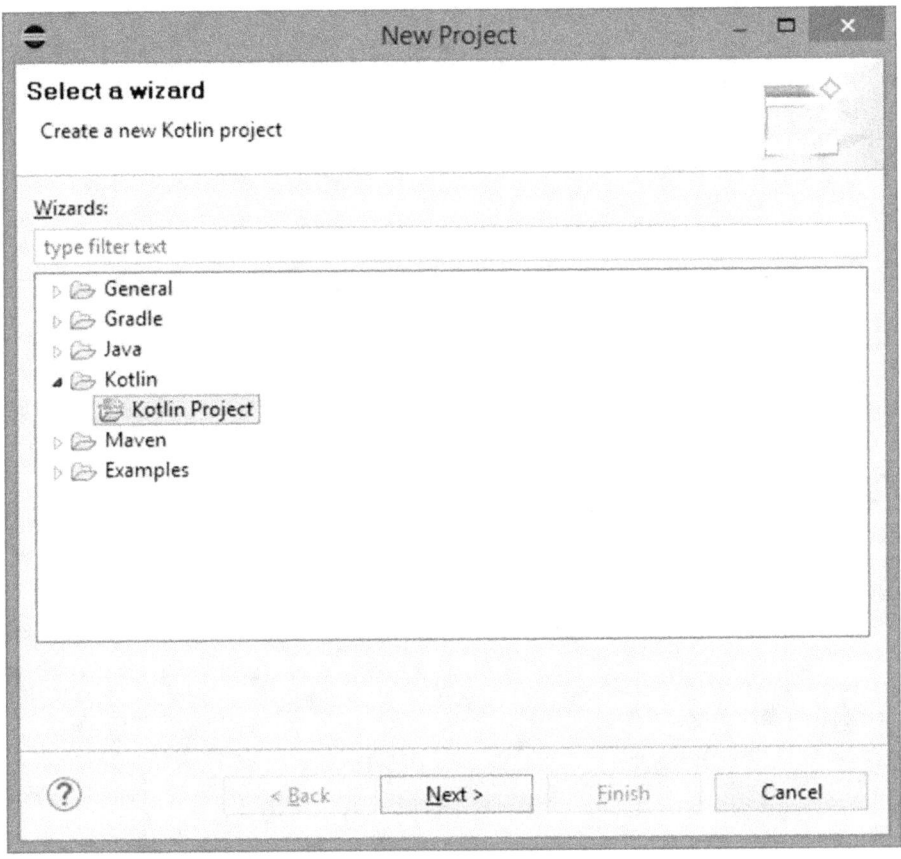

Under *Kotlin*, select *Kotlin Project* and click *Next*.

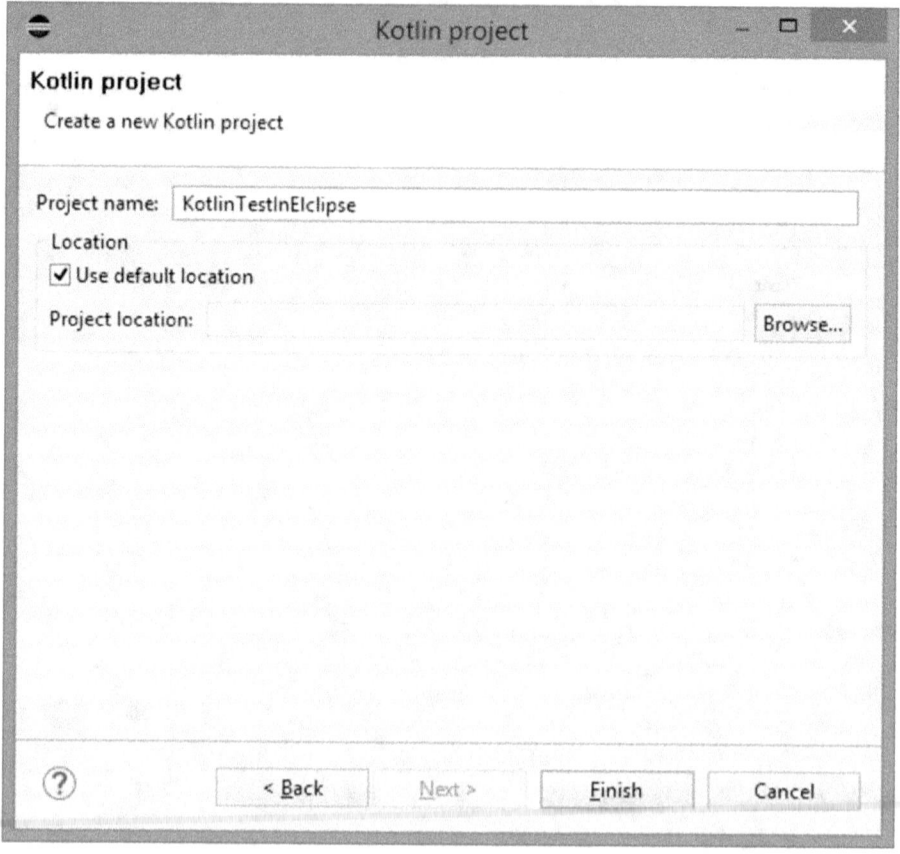

Give your project a name, avoid spaces. Click **Finish**. This will create a new directory with your project's name inside the selected Workspace. Project's directory and its files and sub-directories will be listed under **Package Explorer**.

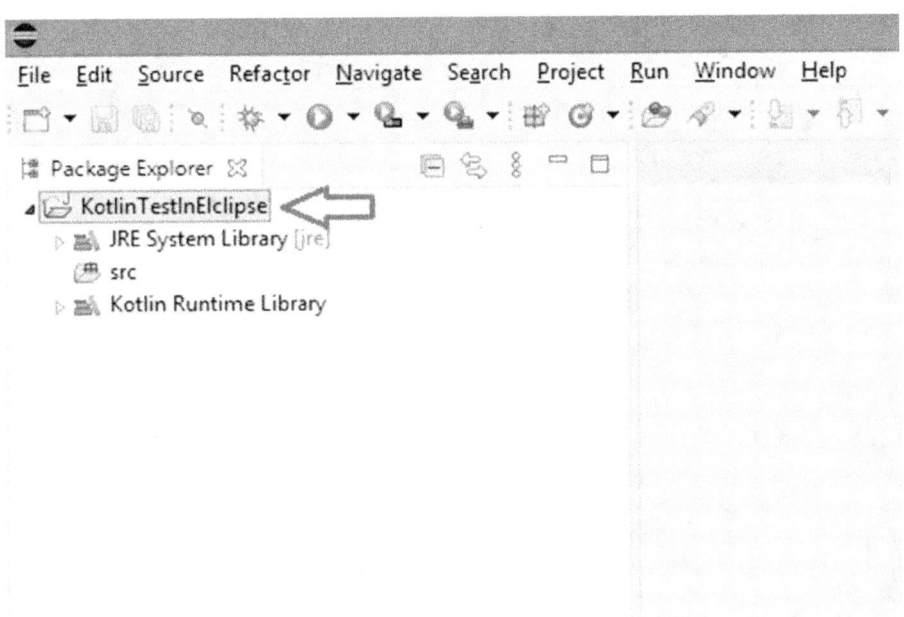

You will be placing Kotlin programs under the *src* directory. Right click on *src*, select *New -> File*.

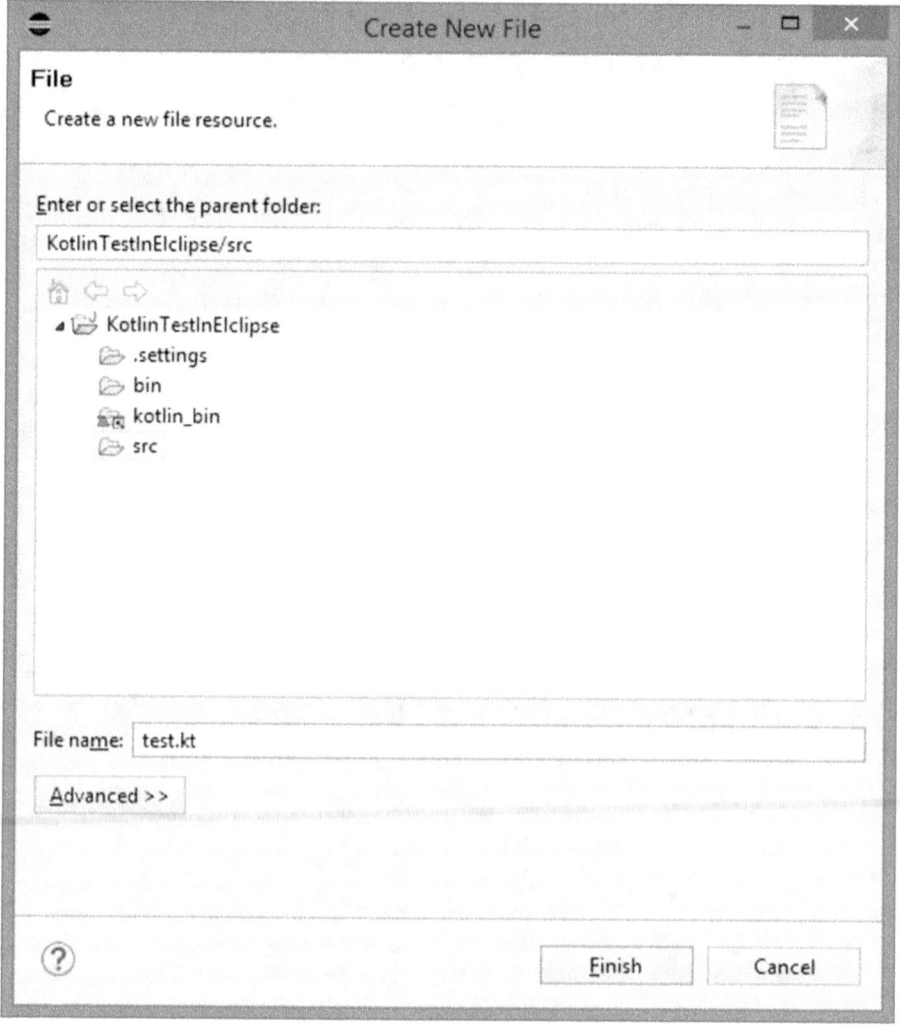

Give your source file a name (with the extension .kt) and click **Finish**. This will create a new file under the **src** directory. Double click on it inside the Package Explorer and it will open in a built-in text editor of Eclipse.

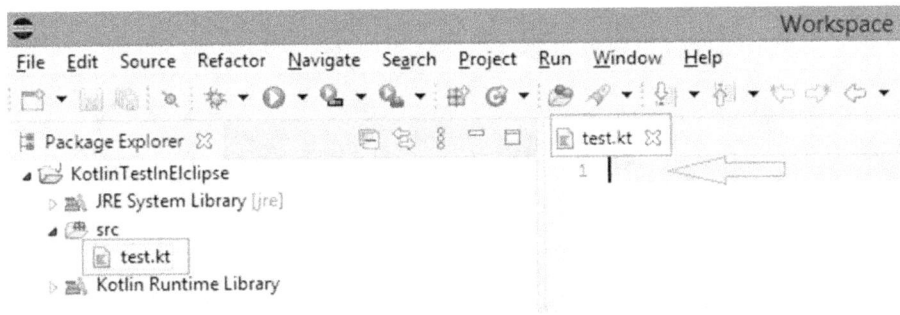

Copy-paste the program from *Section 4.1* into this *.kt* file
and save it. Click on **Run -> Run** from the menu bar. A console
will open at the bottom half of the screen and you will see the
output:

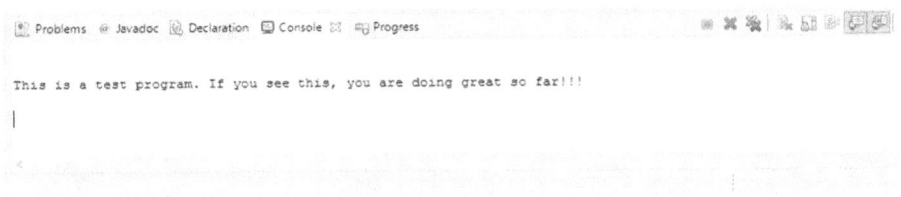

Note: Two different methods of building Kotlin applications
are covered in this chapter – using Kotlin compiler and using
IDEs (Intellij IDEA and Eclipse). Which method you use is not
that important. You should always stick to the operating system
and development tools that your are most comfortable with.
Most programs in this book are compiled using the command
line Kotlin compiler. Having said that, it is also worth noting
again that most of the Kotlin development that is happening in
the industry is geared towards Android application development
and web application development. For such things, you have you
have to use IDEs.

5. Syntax

Kotlin is a case-sensitive programming language. This means that the words "Kotlin", "koTlin" and "kotlin" are treated differently. This chapter onward, we will be learning the actual programming concepts.

5.1 Statements

A statement in Kotlin is used to perform a task or a group of tasks. A task can be anything such as declaring a variable, printing something on the screen, reading from a file, checking for a condition, making a decision, etc. In Kotlin, one statement is present on one line. Here are some examples of statements:

var name: String = "Liza"
println ("Hello")
$y = m * x + c$

5.2 Comments

Comments are ignored by the compiler and have absolutely no effect on the outcome of a program. Kotlin supports single line comments as well as multi-line comments. Single line comments begin with **two forward slashes (//)** and has to begin and end on the same line. Here is an example:

//This is a single line comment

A multi-line comment can span across more than one lines. It begins with a **forward slash and asterisk (/*)** and ends with **asterisk and forward slash (*/)**. Here is an example:

/ This is a multi-line comment.*

It can span across multiple line.

*This line is also a part of the same multi-line comment */*

Note: There are no hard and fast rules related to when and how to use comments. Normally, comments are used to mark or explain a piece of code. This book has plenty of programming examples. Each program has been commented well. While learning those programs, go through the comments to better understand the working of a particular program.

5.3 Identifiers

An identifier is a name given to identify a variable, function, class, etc. This name can contain alphabets – in both upper/lower case and numbers but cannot begin with a number. The only special character allowed inside an identifier name is an **underscore (_)**.

5.4 Keywords

Keywords are reserved words and cannot be used as identifier names. Here is a list of all the important keywords in Kotlin:

as	break	class	continue	do	else
false	for	fun	if	in	interface
is	null	object	package	return	super
this	throw	true	try	typealias	typeof
val	var	when	while		

Note: You do not have to know about all these keywords. The important ones will be covered in the relevant sections of this book.

5.5 Basic Kotlin Program Structure

A very basic Kotlin program can work with only a *main function*. This function serves as an entry point to the program. That is, the program will begin execution from the first valid statement inside the main function. Here is how you write a main function:

```
fun main ( ) {
//Statements
}
```

Note: The keyword *fun* which precedes main is a keyword used to define functions.

A Kotlin program written by a professional developer will have a package statement and import statements as follows:

```
package <package name>
import <package name>

...

...

...

fun main ( ) {
//Statements
}
```

6. Hello World! Kotlin Application

So far we have learned how to set set up the Kotlin compiler and IDEs; we have also learned to compile an existing program and run it. In *Section 5.5*, we saw that a simple and valid Kotlin program can be written with just one *main function* in it. Now, let us put together all the concepts we learned so far and a few new ones in order to write a program that prints *"Hello World!"* on the console.

"Hello World!" is a sequence of characters; commonly known as a string in the programming world. There is a function called *println* in Kotlin that prints a given string on the console. All we have to do is understand how to use this function and put it inside the main function. Here is the basic syntax of *println* to print a string on the console:

println (<string enclosed in double quotes>)

Example:

println ("You should see this on the console!")

Let us now write a Kotlin program with a *println* function that prints Hello World! on the console:

```
//This is the first program that we learn to write
//Prints Hello World! on the console
fun main() {
 println("Hello World!")
}
```

Output:

The ***println*** function can make use of escape character sequences such as \ *n* and \ *t* to enter a newline character and leave a tab-space indent respectively. Here is an example:

```kotlin
//Escape character demo
fun main() {
 println("\nEscape character sequence demo:")
 println("\nThis should be printed on a new line.")
 println("\t\tWhile this should be printed at two
 tab-space indents.\n")

}
```

Output:

7. Data Types

When developing an application, we may have to deal with different kinds of data. For example, if we want to develop an application that stores personal information such as name, address, age, etc., name and address would be one kind of data, age would be another kind of data and so on. A *data type* specifies the category of data we are dealing with. Let us take a look at the basic data types offered by Kotlin. The following sections will give you an introduction; how to use data types will be clearer in the *Variables* chapter.

7.1 Strings

A string is a sequence of characters. The data type used to declare a string is *String*. When setting a string variable, characters can be enclosed within double quotes and assigned to a string variable.

7.2 Boolean

A boolean data type can either be *true* or *false*. The data type used to declare a boolean variable is *Boolean*.

7.3 Numbers

Numbers, as the name suggests are used to deal with numeric values. There are sub categories of numbers. The respective data types are – *Int, Short, Long, Byte, Float and Double*.

7.4 Character

A character data type is used to store a single character. The data type to be used is *Char*. When assigning values to a character variable, a character can be enclosed within single quotes.

Alongside these basic types, there are more data types which support a collection of items such as arrays and ranges. More details on those types will be covered in the relevant chapters. Also, Kotlin being an object oriented programming language, it supports user defined data types using classes and objects. There are a few chapters on OOP concepts later in this book.

8. Variables

A variable is a name given to a memory location. When we store data in a program – for example, name of a person, it is stored at a uniquely addressable memory location. Memory locations are addressed using hexadecimal values. Variables provide an easy way to handle data using variable names instead of directly dealing with memory location's hexadecimal addresses. In other words, a variable name can be referred to as an alias for a memory address.

8.1 Variable Declaration

A variable can be declared using **var** and **val** keywords. The keywords **var** and **val** are used to declare **mutable** variables and **immutable** variables respectively. Mutable variables are those whose values can be changed through the course of the program where as values of immutable variables can be set only once and cannot be changed through the course of the program. Variable naming rules are the same as any other identifier naming rules – a variable name can contain alphanumeric characters, cannot begin with a number, no special characters are permitted except for underscore and reserved keywords cannot be used as variable names. Here is a general syntax of declaring variables:

var <variable name>: <Data Type>
val <variable name>: <Data Type>

Example:

var name: String
var Person_address: String

val age: Int

val gender: Char

8.2 Variable Assignment

The **equal to sign** (=) is the de-facto assignment operator in Kotlin. It assigns the value of the operand on the right to the operand on the left. Here are a few examples of variable assignment:

var name: String

var Person_address: String

val age: Int

name = "Carly"

Person_address = "NYC"

age = 33

Notes:

1. A variable must be declared first before it is assigned.

2. An immutable variable can be set only once. In the above example, age is an immutable variable which is set to 33. If we try to reassign a different value to this variable, the compiler will return an error.

8.3 Variable Initialization

Variables can be initialized at the time of declaration using the following syntax:

var <variable name>: <Data Type> = <Initial Value>

val <variable name>: <Data Type> = <Initial Value>

Example:

var name: String = "Fido"
val gender: Char = 'M'

Variable initialization can also be done without specifying a data type as follows:

var <variable name> = <Initial Value>
val <variable name> = <Initial Value>

Example:

var name = "Queeny"
var gender = 'F'

8.4 Printing Variables Contents

The contents of a variable can be printed using the ***println*** function. The variable name prefixed with ***dollar sign ($)*** can be inserted inside the string to be printed. Here is the general syntax:

println("$<variable>")

Example:

var first_name = "Rudolf"
var age = 29
println("Your name is $first_name and you are $age years old")

Let us put these concepts to use and write a few Kotlin programs. Here is a simple one where different kinds of variables are declared, assigned values and then printed:

```
/*Variables Demo 1*/
fun main() {
 /*Declare Variables*/
 var num: Int
```

```kotlin
var name: String
var flag: Boolean
var c: Char
//Assign values to variables
num = 40
name = "Maggie"
flag = true
c = 'Z'
//Print variable values
println("\nnum: $num \nname: $name \nflag: $flag \nc: $c \n")
}
```

Output:

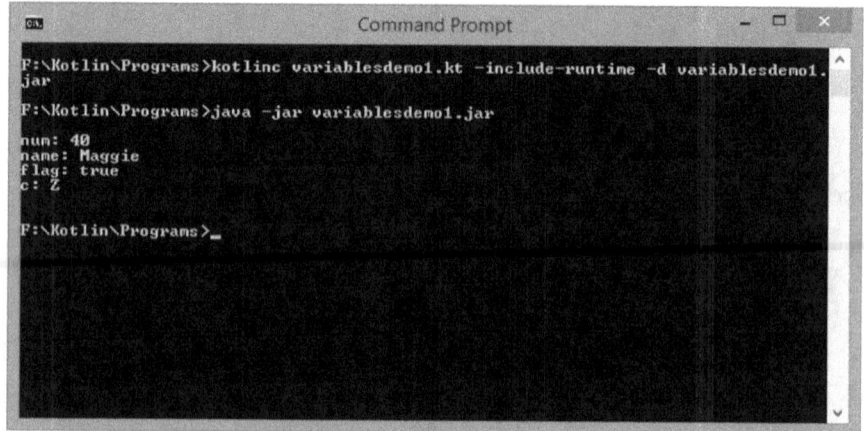

Here is a demo on variable initialization:

```kotlin
/*Variables Demo 2*/
fun main() {
/*Declare and Initialize Variables*/
var height: Double = 5.73
var msg: String = "Home"
var x = 25
//Print variable values
println("\nheight: $height \nmsg: $msg \nx = $x \n")
}
```

Output:

The following programming example demonstrates the usage of *val* keyword:

```kotlin
/*Variables Demo 3*/
fun main() {
 /*Declare and initialize non mutable Variables*/
 val age: Int = 23
 val name: String = "Chris"
 val flag: Boolean = false
 val c: Char = 'G'
 //Print variable values
 println("\nage: $age \nname: $name \nflag: $flag
\nc: $c \n")
 }
```

Output:

Another way of printing variable contents is to used the string concatenation operator given by the plus sign (+). Here is the general syntax:

println(<string 1> + <string 2/variable/value/expression> + ...)

Example:

println("Name: " + name + " Address: " + address + " Age: " + age)

9. Introduction to Object Oriented Programming

Object Oriented Programming (abbreviated as OOP) is a programming paradigm where emphasis is more on the data rather than on the procedure. OOP is a vast concept and covering everything is beyond the scope of this book. There are two very important concepts in OOP – *classes and objects*. This chapter will give you a basic understanding of what are classes and objects. There is another chapter in this book towards the end called *Introduction to Classes and Objects* which deals with actual programming concepts while this chapter will be theoretical. The reason behind placing the current chapter here is because some of the following chapters make use of OOP concepts and hence it is important that you know the basics of OOP before moving ahead.

A *class* is a user defined data type – a collection of *variables* known as *data members, attributes or properties* and *functions* that work on these data members known as *member functions*. A class is simply a blue print of how the custom data type looks like. It may or may not contain any data on its own.

An *object* is an instance of a class having its own set of *data members/attributes/properties* and *member functions* as defined in the class.

Let us understand the concept of classes and objects with the help of an example. Consider that we want to store details about people. A person can have details such as name, age, gender, country, etc. We can create a class called *Person* having properties –

name, age, gender and country. The class Person is just a definition of a user defined data type and does not contain any data. An object of class Person will refer to an actual person and will have its own set of properties – *name, age, gender and country*. Refer to the following diagram:

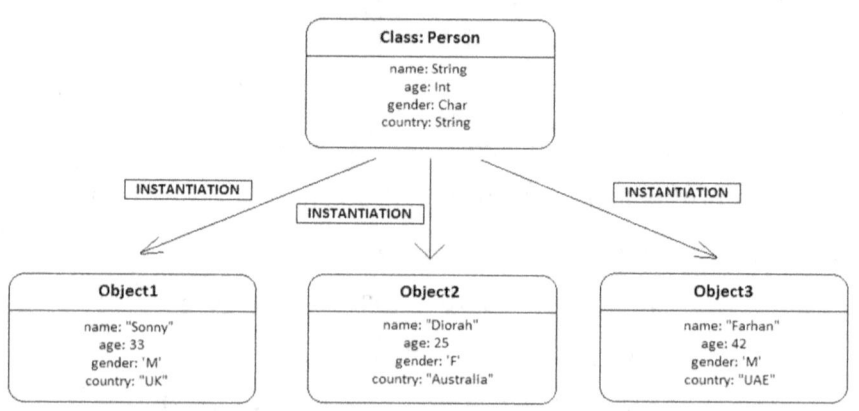

As mentioned earlier, we see that there is a class called Person and it has the following data members – *name (type String), age (type Int), gender (type Char)* and *country (type String)*. Three objects of class Person are created – *Object1, Object2* and *Object3*. These objects have their own copies of data members. For example, Object1 has its name property set to "Sonny" while Object2 has its name property set to "Diorah". In simple terms, we can say that an object of type Person class refers to an actual person whose data is being stored.

9.1 Accessing Data Members/Member functions

Data members and member functions of an object can be accessed using the *dot (.) operator.* General syntax:

<Object/Class>.<Data Member/Member Function>

Eg:

import kotlin.Math

...

...

var x:= Math.tan(3.14 / 2)

//Math is a class and tan is a member function of the Math class which calculates the trigonometric tangent of a given angle (radians).

A class can be defined inside another class. This process is called nesting of classes. In order to access the inner classes, you will have to use multiple dot operators in one statement.

10. Operators

An operator is a symbol or a group of symbols used to perform some kind of an operation. Kotlin offers these operators – arithmetic operators, relational operators, unary operators, logical operators and assignment operators. Let us take a look at each category of operators.

10.1 Arithmetic Operators

An arithmetic operator are used to perform arithmetic operations such as addition, subtractions, multiplication, etc.

Operator	Description	Sample Usage	Explanation
+	Addition	x + y	Performs arithmetic addition, returns sum of the operands.
-	Subtraction	x - y	Subtracts operand on the right from the operand on the left and returns the difference.
*	Multiplication	x * y	Multiplies all operands and returns the product.
/	Division	x / y	Divides the operand on the left by the operand on the right and returns the quotient.
%	Modulus	x % y	Divides the operand on the left by the operand on the right and returns the remainder. Operands needs to be of integer type.

Here is a Kotlin program that demonstrates the usage of arithmetic operators:

```kotlin
/*Arithmetic Operators*/
fun main() {
 //Declare some variables and initialize them
 val num1: Int = 21
 val num2: Int = 8
 var sum: Int
 var diff: Int
 var prod: Int
 var mod: Int
 var quo: Int
 //Perform arithmetic operations
 sum = num1 + num2
 diff = num1 - num2
 prod = num1 * num2
 quo = num1 / num2
 mod = num1 % num2
 //Print everything
 println("\nnum1 = $num1 \nnum2 = $num2")
 println("\nnum1 + num2 = $sum")
 println("num1 - num2 = $diff")
 println("num1 * num2 = $prod")
 println("num1 / num2 = $quo")
 println("num1 % num2 = $mod")
}
```

Output:

10.2 Relational Operators

Relational operators, also known as comparison operators are used to compare operands and determine whether an operand is greater than the other operand, whether two operands are equal and so on. The result of such comparison can either be *true* or *false*.

Operator	Description	Sample Usage	Explanation
==	Equal To	x == y	Returns *true* if both operands are *EQUAL*, *false* otherwise.
!=	Not Equal To	x != y	Returns *true* if both operands are *NOT EQUAL*, *false* otherwise.
<	Less Than	x < y	Returns *true* if the value of the left operand is less than the value of the operand on the right, returns *false* otherwise.
>	Greater Than	x > y	Returns *true* if the value of the left operand is greater than the value of the right operand, *false* otherwise.
<=	Less Than OR Equal To	x <= y	Returns true if the value of the left operand is less than *OR EQUAL TO* the value of the operand on the right, *false* otherwise.
>=	Greater Than OR Equal To	x >= y	Returns *true* if the value of the left operand is greater than *OR EQUAL TO* the value of the operand on the right, *false* otherwise.

Here is a Kotlin program that demonstrates the usage of relational operators:

```
/*Relational Operators*/
fun main() {
 //Declare some variables and initialize them
 val num1: Double = -3.53
 val num2: Double = 9.58
 val num3: Double = -3.53
 //Perform comparison operations and display using
 println
 println("\nnum1 = $num1 num2 = $num2 num3 = $num3")
 println("\nnum1 == num3: "+ (num1 == num3))
 println("\nnum1 != num2: "+ (num1 != num2))
 println("\nnum2 < num3: "+ (num2 < num3))
 println("\nnum1 > num3: "+ (num1 > num3))
 println("\nnum1 <= num2: "+ (num1 < num2))
 println("\nnum3 >= num1: "+ (num3 >= num1))
 }
```

Output:

```
F:\Kotlin\Programs>kotlinc relationaloperators.kt -include-runtime -d relational
operators.jar

F:\Kotlin\Programs>java -jar relationaloperators.jar

num1 = -3.53 num2 = 9.58 num3 = -3.53

num1 == num3: true

num1 != num2: true

num2 < num3: false

num1 > num3: false

num1 <= num2: true

num3 >= num1: true

F:\Kotlin\Programs>
```

10.3 Unary Operators

Unary operators work on a single operand; hence the name. These operators are used to increment or decrement an operand.

Operator	Description	Sample Usage	Explanation
++	Increment	x++ ++x	Increments the given operand. In case of pre-increment (++x), the operand will be incremented first and then used in an expression. In case of post-increment (x++), the value of the operand will be used first in an expression and then incremented.
--	Decrement	y-- --y	Decrements the given operand. In case of pre-decrement (--y), the operand will be decremented first and then used in an expression. In case of post-decrement (y--), the value of the operand will be used first in an expression and then decremented.

Let us write a program to see how unary operators work:

```
/*Unary Operators*/
fun main() {
//Declare some variables and infantilize them
var x: Int = 26
var y: Int = 82
//Print everything and demonstrate inc dec
operations
println("\nx = $x y = $y")
```

```
println("\nPost   Increment:\nx++  =   "+  (x++)   +"\nx
(now, after post inc) = $x")
println("\nPre Increment:\n++y = "+ (++y) +"\ny (now,
after pre inc) = $y")
println("\nCurrrent values:\n\nx = $x y = $y")
println("\nPost   Decrement:\nx--  =   "+  (x--)   +"\nx
(now, after post dec) = $x")
println("\nPre Decrement:\n--y = "+ (--y) +"\ny (now,
after pre dec) = $y")
}
```

Output:

10.4 Logical Operators

Logical operators are used to carry out logical operations such as logical **AND**, logical **OR** and logical **NOT**.

Operator	Description	Sample Usage	Explanation
&&	Logical AND	(Expression X) && (Expression Y)	Returns **true** if all the expressions evaluate to **true**. Returns **false** if any one of the expressions evaluate to **false**.
||	Logical OR	(Expression X) && (Expression Y)	Returns **true** if any one of the expressions evaluate to **true**. Returns **false** if all of the expressions evaluate to **false**.
!	Logical NOT	!(Expression)	Inverts the evaluation of the expression. If the expression evaluates to **true**, **false** will be returned and if the operand is **false**, **true** will be returned.

Here is a program that demonstrates the usage of logical operators:

```
/*Logical Operators*/
fun main() {
//Declare some variables and initialize them
val num1: Int = 5
val num2: Int = -7
val num3: Int = 18
val flag: Boolean = false
//Perform logical operations and display using println
println("\nnum1 = $num1 num2 = $num2 num3 = $num3 flag = $flag")
```

```
println("\n(num1  ==  num2)  &&  (num3 > num2):  "+
((num1 == num2) && (num3 > num2)))
println("\n(num1  <  num3)  ||  (num2 > num3 ):  "+
((num1 < num3) || (num2 > num3)))
println("\n!(flag): "+ (!(flag)))
}
```

Output:

10.5 Assignment Operators

We have seen the default assignment operator given by the equal to sign. Here are a few more assignment operators.

Operator	Description	Sample Usage	Equivalent To
+=	Perform addition and assign sum to the operand on the left.	x += y	x = x + y
-=	Subtract operand on the right from the operand on the left and assigns difference to the operand on the left.	x -= y	x = x − y
*=	Multiplies operands and assigns product to the operand on the left.	x *= y	x = x * y
/=	Divides the operand on the left by the operand on the right and assigns quotient to the operand on the left.	x /= y	x = x / y
%=	Divides the operand on the left by the operand on the right and assigns remainder to the operand on the left.	x %= y	x = x % y

The following program shows how to use these operators:

```
/*Assignment Operators*/
fun main() {
//Declare some variables and initialize them
var num1: Int = -6
var num2: Int = 8
var num3: Int = -12
var num4: Int = 23
```

```
//Perform assignment operations
println("\nnum1 = $num1 num2 = $num2 num3 = $num3
num4 = $num4")
num1 += num2
println("\nPerformed: num1 += num2 ==> num1 = $num1")
num3 -= num4
println("\nPerformed: num3 -= num4 ==> num3 = $num3")
num1 *= num3
println("\nPerformed: num1 *= num3 ==> num1 = $num1")
num2 /= num1
println("\nPerformed: num2 /= num1 ==> num2 = $num2")
num4 %= num1
println("\nPerformed: num4 %= num1 ==> num4 = $num4")
}
```

Output:

10.6 Bitwise Operators

Bitwise operators work on the individual bits of the operands. In order to understand this class of operators, basic knowledge of binary number system and boolean algebra is required. The usage of these operators make use of OOP concepts where the operand is an object and the operator is a member function which works on the object.

Operator	Description	Sample Usage	Explanation
shl	Shift Left	a.shl(b)	Left shift bits of a by b times.
shr	Right Shift	a.shr(b)	Right shift bits of a by b times.
ushr	Unsigned Shift Right	a.ushr(b)	Right shift bit of a by b times (unsigned).
and	Bitwise Logical AND	a.and(b)	Performs a (AND) b
or	Bitwise Logical OR	a.or(b)	Performs a (OR) b
xor	Bitwise Logical XOR	a.xor(b)	Performs a (XOR) b
inv	Invert	a.inv()	Inverts the bits of the given operand. That is, calculates 1's compliment.

Here is a program that demonstrates the usage of bitwise operators:

```
/*Bitwise Operators*/
fun main() {
//Declare some variables and initialize them
var num1: Int = 19
var num2: Int = -34
//Perform    bitwise    operations    and    display
simultaneously
println("\nnum1 = $num1 num2 = $num2")
println("\nSigned Left Shift $num1 by 3 positions: "
+ num1.shl(3))
println("\nSigned Right Shift $num2 by 2 positions:
" + num1.shr(2))
println("\nUnsigned Right Shift $num2 by 1 positions:
" + num1.ushr(1))
println("\nBitwise AND -> $num1 AND $num2 : " +
num1.and(num2))
println("\nBitwise OR -> $num1 OR $num2 : " +
num1.or(num2))
println("\nBitwise XOR -> $num1 XOR $num2 : " +
num1.xor(num2))
println("\nInvert $num1: " + num1.inv())
}
```

Output:

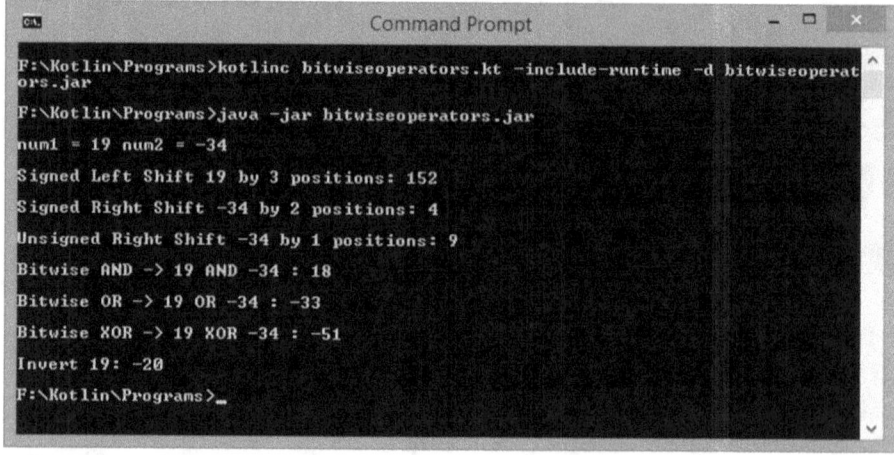

```
F:\Kotlin\Programs>kotlinc bitwiseoperators.kt -include-runtime -d bitwiseoperat
ors.jar

F:\Kotlin\Programs>java -jar bitwiseoperators.jar
num1 = 19 num2 = -34
Signed Left Shift 19 by 3 positions: 152
Signed Right Shift -34 by 2 positions: 4
Unsigned Right Shift -34 by 1 positions: 9
Bitwise AND -> 19 AND -34 : 18
Bitwise OR -> 19 OR -34 : -33
Bitwise XOR -> 19 XOR -34 : -51
Invert 19: -20
F:\Kotlin\Programs>_
```

11. User Interaction

Several basic programming topics have been covered so far. All the programming examples that we have seen never had any sort of user-interaction. Once the programs were compiled and executed, they would run till the last line of code and that was it. In this section, we will learn how to take input from the user.

11.1 Reading Strings

It is very easy to read string input from the user using the *readLine()* function. Here is the general syntax:

<string variable> = readLine()!!

Example:

var msg: String
msg = readLine()!!

The *readLine* function implements a **blocking I/O call**. This means, when the execution control reaches a *readLine* statement, the execution of the program will pause momentarily and give the user an opportunity to enter something through the keyboard. Once the user enters something and presses **Enter**, whatever the user has entered will be fetched (this process is implicit) in string format and returned to the receiving variable. It is only then that execution of the program will proceed. If the user never enters anything, the program will stay there forever unless it is terminated externally.

Note:

- The readLine function will read only in string format. Even if the user enters a number, it will be read in string format.

- The two **exclamation marks (!!)** at the end of the function statement are used to ensure that the input is not **null**.

- The readLine function is present in **kotlin.io** package. A number of packages including this one is included by default when we compile the program with **-include-runtime** compiler option. The appropriate class from this package in turn uses the readLine function from **java.io.BufferedReader** Java class. This is only mentioned for educational purpose, the programmer in most cases will never have to deal with the internals.

Let us take a look at a basic programming example where we will ask the user to enter something and print it back:

```kotlin
/*User Input 1*/
fun main() {
//Declare a variable to store user's input
val msg: String
println("\nEnter some text: ")
//Read using readLine
msg = readLine()!!
//Print back what the user entered
println("\nYou have entered: \n" +msg)
}
```

Output:

Let us write another program and read multiple inputs one by one:

```
/*User Input 2*/
fun main() {
//Declare some variables to store user's input
var name: String
var gender: String
var age: String
var country: String
println("\nEnter your name: ")
//Read using readLine
name = readLine()!!
println("\nEnter your gender: ")
//Read using readLine
gender = readLine()!!
println("\nEnter your age: ")
//Read using readLine
age = readLine()!!
println("\nEnter your country: ")
//Read using readLine
country = readLine()!!
//Print back everything
println("\nYou have entered: \n\nname: $name\ngender:
$gender\nage: $age\ncountry: $country\n")
}
```

Output:

```
C:\Windows\system32\cmd.exe                            _  □  ×

F:\Kotlin\Programs>kotlin userinput2.jar -include-runtime -d userinput2.jar
Enter your name:
Cathy

Enter your gender:
Female

Enter your age:
26

Enter your country:
Norway

You have entered:

name: Cathy
gender: Female
age: 26
country: Norway

F:\Kotlin\Programs>_
```

11.2 Reading Numbers

As mentioned earlier, the readLine function will always read the given input in string format regardless of what the user enters including numbers. There are many ways to read numbers, we will take a look at two of them. The first one is quite straightforward where you read a number in string format using the readLine function and then convert it to the desired numerical format using the appropriate data type conversion functions:

toInt( ) -- For converting a number in string format to *Int.*

toFloat( ) -- For converting a number in string format to *Float.*

toDouble( ) -- For converting a number in string format to *Double.*

These functions are present as member functions in the *String class* and work on string objects (variables). Here is a general syntax of how to use them:

<num variable> = <string variable>.<conversion function>( )

Example:

var x_str: String
var y_str: String
var z_str: String
val x: Int
val y: Float
val z: Double

x_str = "23"
y_str = "5.76"
z_str = "-68.24576"
x = x_str.toInt()
y = y_str.toFloat()
z = z_str.toDouble()

Here is a program that adds two given numbers. The program first asks the user to enter two numbers, reads them as strings using the readLine function, converts them to Int using toInt function and then adds them:

```
/*Integer Input - Add two numbers*/
/*Read input using readLine in string format and
then convert to Int*/
fun main() {
//Declare some variables to store user's input
var num1_str: String
var num2_str: String
val num1: Int
val num2: Int
val sum: Int
println("\nEnter a number: ")
```

```kotlin
//Read using readLine
num1_str = readLine()!!
println("\nEnter another number: ")
//Read using readLine
num2_str = readLine()!!
//Convert the numbers in string format to Int format
num1 = num1_str.toInt()
num2 = num2_str.toInt()
//Calculate sum
sum = num1 + num2
//Print sum
println("\n$num1 + $num2 = $sum \n")
}
```

Output:

```
C:\Windows\system32\cmd.exe                           -  □  ×

F:\Kotlin\Programs>kotlinc addtwonumbers.kt -include-runtime -d addtwonumbers.ja
r
F:\Kotlin\Programs>java -jar addtwonumbers.jar
Enter a number:
234

Enter another number:
792

234 + 792 = 1026

F:\Kotlin\Programs>_
```

Let us write another program to multiply three Float numbers:

```kotlin
/*Float Input - Multiply three numbers*/
/*Read input using readLine in string format and
then convert to Float*/
fun main() {
//Declare some variables to store user's input
var num1_str: String
var num2_str: String
var num3_str: String
val num1: Float
val num2: Float
```

82

```kotlin
    val num3: Float
    val product: Float
    println("\nEnter the first number: ")
    //Read using readLine
    num1_str = readLine()!!
    println("\nEnter the second number: ")
    //Read using readLine
    num2_str = readLine()!!
    println("\nEnter the third number: ")
    //Read using readLine
    num3_str = readLine()!!
    //Convert the numbers in string format to Float
    format
    num1 = num1_str.toFloat()
    num2 = num2_str.toFloat()
    num3 = num3_str.toFloat()
    //Calculate product
    product = num1 * num2 * num3
    //Print product
    println("\n$num1 x $num2 x $num3 = $product \n")
}
```

Output:

The other method of reading numbers is slightly cumbersome but is efficient and a preferred method. This method makes use of the *Scanner class* from the *java.util* package. Hence, any

Kotlin program that uses this method will have to include the *java.util.Scanner* class. This can be done using the *import* statement as follows:

import java.util.Scanner

Moving forward, a scanner object must be declared which specifies the input stream. We will be using the **System. `in`** which is the standard input stream. This input stream is responsible for fetching input from the keyboard. Here is how to declare the scanner object:

val <scanner object> = Scanner (System. `in`)

Example:

val number_scanner = Scanner (System. `in`)

Once the scanner object is declared, functions form the Scanner class can be used to read specific types of numbers:

nextInt() -- Read number in **Int** format.
nextFloat() -- Read number in **Float** format.
nextDouble() -- Read number in **Double** format.

Here is how you would use these functions:

import java.util.Scanner
fun main () {
val num_scanner = Scanner(System. `in`)
var x: Int
var y: Float
var z: Double
println("\nEnter an integer, float and double respectively: ")

$$x = num\_scanner.nextInt\ (\ )$$

$$y = num\_scanner.nextFloat\ (\ )$$

$$z = num\_scanner.nextDouble\ (\ )$$

$$println("\backslash nx = \$x\ y = \$y\ z = \$z")$$

$$\}$$

Let us write a program to read two Double values from the user using the scanner class and calculate their sum, difference, product and quotient:

```
/*Double Input - Using java.util.Scanner class*/
import java.util.Scanner
fun main() {
//Declare some variables
var num1: Double
var num2: Double
var sum: Double
var diff: Double
var prod: Double
var quo: Double
//Declare Scanner object
val num_scanner = Scanner(System.`in`)
//Prompt the user to enter two numbers, one by one
println("\nEnter a number: ")
//Read using Scanner class
num1 = num_scanner.nextDouble()
println("\nEnter another number: ")
//Read using Scanner class
num2 = num_scanner.nextDouble()
//Perform arithmetic operations
sum = num1 + num2
diff = num1 - num2
prod = num1 * num2
quo = num1 / num2
//Print everything
```

```kotlin
println("\nSum = $sum \nDifference = $diff \nProduct
= $prod \nQuotient = $quo \n")
}
```

Output:

```
C:\Windows\system32\cmd.exe

F:\Kotlin\Programs>kotlinc scannerinput.kt -include-runtime -d scannerinput.jar

F:\Kotlin\Programs>java -jar scannerinput.jar

Enter a number:
56.258701

Enter another number:
38.930175

Sum = 95.188876
Difference = 17.328526000000004
Product = 2190.161075202675
Quotient = 1.4451181121071253

F:\Kotlin\Programs>
```

12. Flow Control

All the programming examples that we have seen so far had a linear flow of execution. That is, a syntactically correct program would execute from the first statement to the last one. If you want to alter this linear flow of execution, you can make use of control structures.

Control structures are programming constructs that exercise control over the execution of a program. Kotlin offers control structures in the form of decision making constructs and loops. These constructs enable programmers introduce an element of conditionality in their code. We will take a look at these categories one by one.

12.1 Decision Making

In Kotlin, decision making constructs are available in the form of if-else and when statements.

12.1.1 If-Else Construct

A simplest form of decision making construct can be realized using an if-statement.

The general syntax is:

if (<condition>) {
//Statements to be executed if <condition> is true.
}
Example:

```
if (num > 0) {
println("\n $num is positive.\n")
}
```

An *if statement* should be given a condition, marked by *<condition>* in the above code snippet. When the execution control encounters an if statement, the supplied condition will be evaluated. A condition is usually a *boolean expression* which either evaluates to *true* or *false*. If the condition evaluates to true, the statements present inside the if block (enclosed within curly brackets { }) will be executed one by one. Where as, if the condition evaluates to false, the if block will be ignored; the execution control will simply skip this block.

Let us take a simple example where we will ask the user to enter a number and check if it is greater than 10:

```kotlin
/*If demo*/
import java.util.Scanner
fun main() {
//Declare some variables
var num: Int
//Declare Scanner object
val num_scanner = Scanner(System.`in`)
//Prompt the user to enter two numbers, one by one
println("\nEnter a number: ")
//Read using Scanner class
num = num_scanner.nextInt()
//Check if the number is greater than 10
if (num > 10) {
println("\n$num is greater than 10.\n")
}
}
```

Output:

As seen from the output, if the user enters a number that is greater than 10, the correct message is displayed. However, if a number less than 10 is entered, nothing happens, the program just exist. That is because, we have not written a piece of code that should get executed if the given condition evaluates to false. An **else statement** lets you handle such situations. Here is the general syntax of how to use an else statement:

if (<condition>) {

// Statements to be executed if <condition> is true.

}

else {

// Statements to be executed if <condition> is false.

}

Example:

if (num > 10) {

println("\n$num is greater than 10.\n")

}

else {

println("\n$num is not greater than 10\n")

}

In case there is an if-else block combination, the condition of the if statement will be evaluated. If it is true, the if block will be executed and the else block will be skipped. If the condition evaluates to false, the if block will be skipped and the else block will be executed.

Here is a program that demonstrates the usage of if and else blocks combined. The program asks the user to enter a number and checks whether or not it is a multiple of 5.

```kotlin
/*If-Else demo*/
import java.util.Scanner
fun main() {
//Declare some variables
var num: Int
//Declare Scanner object
val num_scanner = Scanner(System.`in`)
//Prompt the user to enter two numbers, one by one
println("\nEnter a number: ")
//Read using Scanner class
num = num_scanner.nextInt()
//Check if the number is divisible by 5 using %
operator
if ((num % 5) == 0) {
println("\n$num is a multiple of 5.\n")
}
//If it is not divisible by 5, this block will be
activated
else {
println("\n$num is not a multiple of 5.\n")
}
}
```

Output:

One if-else block combination will let you check for the validity of one condition and will let you do something if the condition is valid or do something else if it is invalid. If you want to check for multiple conditions, you can use the **else-if statement**. Multiple else-if blocks can be sandwiched between the if-block and the else-block. Where each else-if statement will have a condition of its own. Here is a general syntax of how to use if-else if-else block combination:

if (<condition 1>) {

//This block will be executed if <condition 1> is true.

}

else if (<condition 2>) {

//This block will be executed if <condition 1> is false <condition 2> is true.

<statements>

}

else if (<condition 3>) {

//This block will be executed if <condition 1> and <condition 2> are false and <condition 3> is true.

```
        <statements>
    }
    ....
    ....
    ....
```

//Can sandwich as many else-if statements before the else block

else {

   //This block will be executed if <condition 1>, <condition 2>, <condition 3> and   <condition n> all are false.

   }

How this works is — there will be a mandatory if block and there could be several else if blocks, each else if statement having its own condition. The condition of the if statement will be evaluated first. If it evaluates to true, the if block will be executed and rest of the blocks will be skipped. If the condition evaluates to false, the control will go to the following else if block and its condition will be evaluated. If that condition evaluates to true, that else if block will be executed and rest of the blocks will be skipped. This process will continue until an else if block is found whose condition evaluates to true. If no such block is found, the else block (if present) will be executed.

It is time to combine all that we have learned in this section and write a program to check whether a given number is positive, negative or zero:

```
/*If-Else If-Else demo - positive negative zero*/
import java.util.Scanner
fun main() {
//Declare some variables
```

```kotlin
var num: Int
//Declare Scanner object
val num_scanner = Scanner(System.`in`)
//Prompt the user to enter two numbers, one by one
println("\nEnter a number: ")
//Read using Scanner class
num = num_scanner.nextInt()
if (num > 0) {
println("\n$num is positive.\n")
}
else if (num < 0) {
println("\n$num is negative.\n")
}
else {
println("\n$num is zero.\n")
}
}
```

Output:

Note:

- An if statement can be stand-alone while else if and else statements require a preceding if statement.

- if and else if statements allow to specify a condition while there is no way to specify a condition for an else statement.

- An if block can be followed by else if blocks or an else block. No other programming statements are permitted between blocks.

- In one if-else if-else bock combination, only one block will get executed.

- In case there is only one statement inside an if, else if or else block, it need not be enclosed within curly brackets.

- It is possible to nest an if-else block inside another if-else block.

12.1.2 When Construct

The **when construct** works like a **switch-case construct** from programming languages such as C, C++, Java, etc. It is very useful in handling situations where there could be multiple outcomes. Here is the general syntax:

```
when (<expression>) {
    [constant expression 1] -> {
        //Statements to be executed if <expression> matches
[constant expression 1]
    }
```

```
[constant expression 2] -> {
        //Statements to be executed if <expression> matches
[constant expression 2]
        }
        [constant expression 3] -> {
        //Statements to be executed if <expression> matches
[constant expression 3]
        }
        ...
        ...
        ...
        [constant expression n] -> {
        //Statements to be executed if <expression> matches
[constant expression n]
        }
        else -> {
        //Statements to be executed if <expression> does not
match any of the constant expressions.
        }
    }
```

A when statement is given an expression, marked by
<expression> in the above code snippet. There can be several
constant expressions inside the when block, marked by *[constant
expression n]*. The given expression is evaluated and the process of
finding the matching constant expression begins. If the evaluation
of *<expression>* matches *[constant expression 1]*, the block of
[constant expression 1] will be executed and rest of the blocks will

be skipped; if not, the next constant expression will be checked. This process will go on until a matching constant expression is found. If no match is found, the else block will be executed; this is like *default case block* from *switch-case construct.*

Let us write a program to check whether a given number is odd or even using *when construct.*

```kotlin
/*When NOT as Expression Demo -- odd or even*/
import java.util.Scanner
fun main() {
 //Declare some variables
 var num: Int
 //Declare Scanner object
 val num_scanner = Scanner(System.`in`)
 //Prompt the user to enter a number
 println("\nEnter a number: ")
 //Read using Scanner class
 num = num_scanner.nextInt()
 //Switch based on num % 2
 when (num % 2) {
     //If the remainder is zero, the number is even
     0 -> {
         println("\n$num is even.\n")
     //If the remainder is one, the number is odd
     }
     1 -> {
         println("\n$num is odd.\n")
     }
     //This is a mandatory block, has no role to
play in the logic of the program
     else -> {
         println("\nInvalid Input.\n")
     }
   }
 }
```

Output:

It is possible to execute the same block of code if the expression can match any of the given constant expressions. The constant expressions will have to be separated by commas in this case. Let us write a program to check whether a given character is a vowel or a consonant:

```kotlin
/*When NOT as Expression Demo*/
import java.util.Scanner
fun main() {
 //Declare a variable
 var c: Char
 //Declare Scanner object
 val char_scanner = Scanner(System.`in`)
 //Prompt the user to enter a character
 println("\nEnter a character: ")
 //Read using Scanner class
 c = char_scanner.next().single()
 //Switch based on c
 when (c) {
    'a','e','i','o','u','A','E','I','O','U' -> {
       println("\n$c is a vowel.\n")
    }
    else -> {
```

```
println("\n$c is a consonant.\n")
    }
  }
}
```

Output:

There is another way of using the when construct – as an expression. Here is the general syntax:

\<variable\> = when (\<expression\>) {

    [constant expression 1] -> [value 1]

    [constant expression 2] -> [value 2]

    [constant expression 3] -> [value 3]

    ...

    ...

    ...

    [constant expression n] -> [value n]

    else -> [value]

}

In this method, each constant expression has a corresponding value, marked by *[value n]* in the above code snippet. When a matching expression is found, the corresponding value is assigned to the *<variable>*. If no match is found, the corresponding value of *else* will be assigned to the *<variable>*.

Let us write a program where we will read the chronological number of the day of a week — 1 for Sunday, 2 for Monday, ... 7 for Saturday and tell the user which day it is:

```kotlin
/*When as Expression Demo*/
import java.util.Scanner
fun main() {
 //Declare some variables
 var num: Int
 val day: String
 //Declare Scanner object
 val num_scanner = Scanner(System.`in`)
 //Prompt the user to enter a number
 println("\nEnter day (1-7 for Sunday to Saturday):
")
 //Read using Scanner class
 num = num_scanner.nextInt()
 //Switch based on num, return string value in day
 day = when (num) {
        1 -> "Sunday"
        2 -> "Monday"
        3 -> "Tuesday"
        4 -> "Wednesday"
        5 -> "Thursday"
        6 -> "Friday"
        7 -> "Saturday"
        else -> "Invalid Input"
 }
 if ((num >= 1) && (num <= 7)) {
```

```
        println("\nThe day is $day\n")
    }
    else {
        println("\n$day\n")
    }
}
```

Output:

12.2 Loops

Loops are programming constructs used to run a piece of code over a number of times. Kotlin offers **while, do while and for loops**. Out of these, we will learn **while** and **do while** in this section; **for loop** will be covered in the arrays chapter as it needs some knowledge of how collections work.

12.2.1 while Loop

The **while loop** is one of the simplest loops you will ever come across. Here is the general syntax:

```
while (<condition>) {
    // Statements to be executed as long as the <condition> is true.
}
```

Example:

```
var count: Int = 0
while (count < 5) {
    println ("Hello while loop!")
    count++
}
```

A while loop should be give a condition marked by **<condition>** in the above code snippet. Just like the condition given to an if-statement this condition is also a boolean expression in most cases which can evaluate to either **true** or **false**. If the condition evaluates to true, the statements inside the while block are executed one by one. This is one *loop iteration*. Once end of the block is reached, the control jumps back to the while statement where the condition is checked again. If it evaluates to true again, the block is executed once again. This process goes on continuing as long the given condition evaluates to true. If the condition never evaluates to false, the loop will go on executing unless the process is terminated externally; such a loop is known as an *infinite loop*. Normally, a *loop variable* is used to keep track of the number of iterations. The said variable is initialized before the loop and incremented/decremented inside the loop as per requirement. This is just one programming technique and not a requirement of the loop itself.

Let us write a program to print numbers from 0 to 9 using a while loop:

```
/*While Demo*/
fun main() {

    //Declare and initialize a loop variable/counter
    var count: Int = 0
    //Loop from 0 to 9
    while (count < 10) {
        //Print count
        println("$count")
        //Increment count
        count++
    }
    println("")
}
```

Output:

12.2.2 do while Loop

The *do while loop* works just like a *while loop* with one major difference. Instead of checking the condition at the beginning of the loop, it is checked at the end of the loop block. This means, a do while loop will execute at least once even if the given condition is false for the very first time. Here is the general syntax:

do {
    // Statements to be executed as long as the <condition> is true.
    } while (<condition>);
    Example:
    var count: Int = 1
    do {
        println ("Hello!!!")
        count++
    } while (count <= 10)

Let us write a program to print multiples of 2 from 2 to 20 using do while loop:

```
/*Do-While Demo*/
fun main() {

    //Declare and initialize a loop variable/counter
    var count: Int = 1
    //Loop from 1 to 10
    do {
        //Print count x 2
        println(count * 2)
        //Increment count
        count++
    } while (count <= 10);
    println("")
}
```

Output:

12.2.3 Loop Control

All three loops – while, do while and for (covered in arrays chapter) will go on executing as long as a condition is met. If you want to control the execution of a loop, you can use loop control statements – **break** and **continue**. When a break statement is encountered, the execution of a loop will terminate abruptly regardless of whether or not more iterations are left. Where as when a continue statement is encountered, the current iteration will be skipped; i.e, the statements below the continue statement will be ignored and the loop will move to the next iteration.

Let us write a program to check whether a given number is prime or composite. We will use a loop to run from 2 till the given number. If the loop variable is able to divide the given number, we will exit the loop using **break** statement:

```
/*Prime or Composite*/
import java.util.Scanner
fun main() {
 //Declare some variables
 var num: Int
```

```kotlin
var flag_prime: Boolean = false
var i: Int = 2
//Declare Scanner object
val num_scanner = Scanner(System.`in`)
//Prompt the user to enter a number
println("\nEnter a number: ")
//Read using Scanner class
num = num_scanner.nextInt()
while (i < num) {
    if (num % i == 0) {
            flag_prime = true
            break
    }
i++
}
if (!flag_prime) {
    println("\n$num is prime.\n")
}
else {
    println("\n$num is composite.\n")
}
}
```

Output:

```
F:\Kotlin\Programs>kotlinc primeorcomposite.kt -include-runtime -d primeorcompos
ite.jar
F:\Kotlin\Programs>java -jar primeorcomposite.jar
Enter a number:
25

25 is composite.

F:\Kotlin\Programs>java -jar primeorcomposite.jar
Enter a number:
31

31 is prime.

F:\Kotlin\Programs>java -jar primeorcomposite.jar
Enter a number:
16

16 is composite.

F:\Kotlin\Programs>java -jar primeorcomposite.jar
Enter a number:
11

11 is prime.

F:\Kotlin\Programs>
```

Now, let us see how continue works in action. We will display multiples of 3 between 3 and 90 but will skip printing the number if it also happens to be a multiple of 4:

```kotlin
/*Continue Demo*/
fun main() {

    //Declare and initialize a loop variable/counter
    var count: Int = 0
    //Loop from 1 to 30
    while (count < 30) {
        //Increment count
        count++
        if (count % 4 == 0) {
            continue
        }
        //Print count x 3
        println(count * 3)
    }
    println("")
}
```

Output:

In this chapter, we have learned decision making and loops. Let us combine both these concepts and write a menu driven Kotlin program which gives user a menu for performing arithmetic operations:

```kotlin
/*Menu driven program*/
import java.util.Scanner
fun main() {
 //Declare some variables
 var choice: Int
 var num1: Double
 var num2: Double
 var sum: Double
 var diff: Double
 var prod: Double
 var quo: Double
 //Declare Scanner object
 val num_scanner = Scanner(System.`in`)
 while (true) {
```

```kotlin
    //Display menu Prompt the user to enter their
choice
    println("\n\n1. Addition\n2. Subtraction \n3.
Multiplication \n4. Division \n5. Exit \n\nChoice: ")
    choice = num_scanner.nextInt()
    when (choice) {
        1 -> {
            println("\nEnter a number: ")
            //Read using Scanner class
            num1 = num_scanner.nextDouble()
            println("\nEnter another number: ")
            //Read using Scanner class
            num2 = num_scanner.nextDouble()
            sum = num1 + num2
            println("\nSum = $sum\n")
        }
        2 -> {
            println("\nEnter a number: ")
            //Read using Scanner class
            num1 = num_scanner.nextDouble()
            println("\nEnter another number: ")
            //Read using Scanner class
            num2 = num_scanner.nextDouble()
            diff = num1 - num2
            println("\nDifference = $diff\n")


        }
        3 -> {
            println("\nEnter a number: ")
            //Read using Scanner class
            num1 = num_scanner.nextDouble()
            println("\nEnter another number: ")
            //Read using Scanner class
            num2 = num_scanner.nextDouble()
            prod = num1 * num2
            println("\nProduct = $prod\n")
```

```
                    }
    4 -> {
        println("\nEnter a number: ")
        //Read using Scanner class
        num1 = num_scanner.nextDouble()
        println("\nEnter another number: ")
        //Read using Scanner class
        num2 = num_scanner.nextDouble()
        quo = num1 / num2
        println("\nQuotient = $quo\n")


    }
    5 -> {
        break
    }
    else -> {
        println("\nInvalid Choice!")
    }
        }
    }
}
```

Output (1):

```
Command Prompt - java -jar menudriven.jar

F:\Kotlin\Programs>kotlinc menudriven.kt -include-runtime -d menudriven.jar

F:\Kotlin\Programs>java -jar menudriven.jar

1. Addition
2. Subtraction
3. Multiplication
4. Division
5. Exit

Choice:
3

Enter a number:
2

Enter another number:
6

Product = 12.0


1. Addition
2. Subtraction
3. Multiplication
4. Division
5. Exit
```

Output (2):

```
Command Prompt - java -jar menudriven.jar

1. Addition
2. Subtraction
3. Multiplication
4. Division
5. Exit

Choice:
9

Invalid Choice!

1. Addition
2. Subtraction
3. Multiplication
4. Division
5. Exit

Choice:
2

Enter a number:
12

Enter another number:
7

Difference = 5.0
```

110

13. Functions

A function is a piece of code that can be re-used to do the same task again. Functions are also known as *routines* or *sub-routines.* We have used many built-in functions so far. One of the most used functions is *println*. Someone has written the println function so that developers like us can make use of it to print something on the console. It has all the logic to direct output to the output stream. Imagine how inconvenient it would have been if we had to write the whole printing logic every time we wanted to print something on the console! In this section, we will learn to write our own functions. There are two important concepts when learning functions in any programming language – function definition and function call.

13.1 Function Definition

Function definition is a piece of code which gets the desired work done. A function is defined with the help of the *fun* keyword as follows:

```
fun <Function Name> (<Arguments>): <(Optional) Return Type> {
        //Function Body
        //Statements...
        <(Optional) return Statement>
}
Example:
fun abcFunction() {
        println("Inside abcFunction")
}
```

Here is what the code marking means:

- **Function Name:**

  A function name is the name given to a function. This name is used to call the function. Function naming rules are the same as variable naming rules.

- **Arguments:**

  Arguments are data values passed to the function. For example, when we specify a string to be printed using the println function, that string is passed to the function as an argument.

- **Return Type:**

  In case a function returns a value back to the calling function, a return type specifies the data type of the returned value.

- **Function Body:**

  This is the core part of the function where the actual work is done. In this space, you would implement the logic of the function to get the desired outcome.

- **Return Statement:**

  A *return* statement is used to return a value back to the calling function. General syntax is:

  return <value/variable/expression>

13.2 Function Call

A function definition is just a piece of code sitting idle. It will not execute on its own. In order to make it run, you need to invoke the function by calling it. Here is the general syntax:

<function name>(<arguments>)

Example:

abcFunction()

When a function call is encountered, that particular function will be invoked and once the execution control reaches the end of the function block, the control will jump back to the calling function. Say, **abcFunction** was called from the **main** function, once **abcFunction** finishes executing, the control will jump back to the **main** function, precisely one statement after the function call statement.

Let us understand this basic concept of functions using a programming example. We will write a function called as **simpleFunction** outside the main function and call it from the main function.

```
/*Function Demo*/
//Function definition
fun simpleFunction() {
 //Function body
 println("\nInside simpleFunction\n")
}
//Main function
fun main() {
 println("\nInside   main   function.   Now   calling
simpleFunction.")
```

```
//Call simpleFunction
simpleFunction()
println("\nInside  main  function.  Reached  end  of
program.\n")
}
```

<u>Output:</u>

13.3 Functions with Arguments/Parameters

A function can be written to accept arguments or parameters.
An argument/parameter is a data value that is sent to the
function. Here is a general syntax of how to define a function
that accepts arguments:

*fun <Function Name> (<argument 1>: <Data type 1>, <argument
2>: <Data type 2>, ... <argument n>: <Data type n>): <(Optional)
Return Type> {*
  //Function Body
  //Statements...
  <(Optional) return Statement>
}

Example:

fun xyzFunction(name: String, age: Int, weight: Double) {
  println("$name, $age, $weight")
}

In the above example, a function called **xyzFunction** is defined which accepts three arguments – **name (String type), age (Int type)** and **weight (Double type).** These arguments are available as local variables inside the function. When calling a function that accepts arguments, the exact number of parameters should be passed and in the ordered specified in the function definition. General syntax:

<function name>(<argument 1>, <argument 2>, ... <argument n>)

Example:

xyzFunction("Pablo", 34, 140)

If we visualize the above function call, it will look something like this:

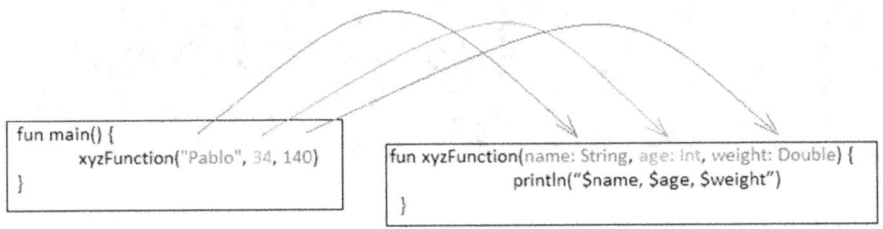

The string **"Pablo"** will be received in **name,** **34** will be received in **age** and **140** will be received in **weight.**

Let us write a program to send arbitrary values to a function and display them:

```
/*Function Demo - Passing arguments*/
//Function definition
fun myFunction(msg: String, num: Int) {
  //Function body
```

```kotlin
    println("\nInside myFunction\n")
    println("\nmsg = $msg \nnum = $num\n")
}
//Main function
fun main() {
    println("\nInside    main    function.    Now    calling
myFunction.")
    //Call myFunction
    myFunction("This is a test message.", 31536)
    println("\nInside    main    function.    Reached    end    of
program.\n")
}
```

Output:

13.4 Returning a value

A function can return a value back to the calling function using the **return** statement. Only one value or variable can be returned. General syntax:

return <variable/value/expression>

Example:

return "Wonderful!"

Note:

- If a function returns a value, the data type of the value that is going to be returned must be specified as the return type of the function. Refer to *Section 12.1.*

- In case an expression is specified, it will be evaluated first and the resultant value will be returned.

When calling a function that returns a value, a variable must be specified to receive the returned value. General syntax:

<variable> = <function>()

Example:

name = getName()

Let us write a function to accept three integers, add them and return their sum. In the main function, we will ask the user to enter three integers and pass them as arguments to the function:

```
/*Function Demo - Add three numbers*/
import java.util.Scanner
//Function definition
fun addNumbers(num1: Int, num2: Int, num3: Int): Int
{
    var sum: Int = num1 + num2 + num3
    return sum
}
//Main function
fun main() {
    var num1: Int
    var num2: Int
    var num3: Int
    var sum: Int
```

```kotlin
val num_scanner = Scanner(System.`in`)
println("\nEnter number 1: ")
//Read using Scanner class
num1 = num_scanner.nextInt()
println("\nEnter number 2: ")
//Read using Scanner class
num2 = num_scanner.nextInt()
println("\nEnter number 3: ")
//Read using Scanner class
num3 = num_scanner.nextInt()
sum = addNumbers(num1, num2, num3)
println("\n$num1 + $num2 + $num3 = $sum \n")
}
```

Output:

Functions is a very important topic in any programming language. Let us take a look at a few more programming examples before proceeding further.

We have learned to carry out basic mathematical operations. We have not come across an operator which is used to raise the power of a number by another number. Let us write a function to raise the power of a base by a given exponent:

```kotlin
/*Function Demo - Power*/
```

```kotlin
//Note: This program will only work for positive
integers.
import java.util.Scanner
//Function definition
fun pow(base: Int, exp: Int): Int {
 var x: Int = 1
 var i: Int = 0
 while (i < exp) {
     x *= base
     i++
 }
 return x
}
//Main function
fun main() {
 var base: Int
 var exponent: Int
 var result: Int
 val num_scanner = Scanner(System.`in`)
 println("\nEnter the base: ")
 //Read using Scanner class
 base = num_scanner.nextInt()
 println("\nEnter exponent: ")
 //Read using Scanner class
 exponent = num_scanner.nextInt()
 result = pow(base, exponent)
 println("\n$base ^ $exponent = $result \n")
}
```

<u>Output:</u>

At the end of *Chapter 11,* we combined decision making and loops to write a menu driven program. Let us rewrite that program using functions. We will write separate functions for addition, subtraction, multiplication and division:

```kotlin
/*Menu driven program using functions*/
import java.util.Scanner
fun getSum(x: Double, y: Double): Double {
 val sum: Double = (x + y)
 return sum
}
fun getDifference(x: Double, y: Double): Double {
 val diff: Double = (x - y)
 return diff
}
fun getProduct(x: Double, y: Double): Double {
 val prod: Double = (x * y)
 return prod
}
fun getQuotient(x: Double, y: Double): Double {
 val quo: Double = (x / y)
 return quo
}
fun main() {
 //Declare some variables
 var choice: Int
 var num1: Double
 var num2: Double
 var sum: Double
 var diff: Double
 var prod: Double
 var quo: Double
 //Declare Scanner object
 val num_scanner = Scanner(System.`in`)
 while (true) {
     //Display menu Prompt the user to enter their
choice
     println("\n\n1. Addition\n2. Subtraction \n3.
Multiplication \n4. Division \n5. Exit \n\nChoice: ")
```

```kotlin
choice = num_scanner.nextInt()
when (choice) {
    1 -> {
        println("\nEnter a number: ")
        //Read using Scanner class
        num1 = num_scanner.nextDouble()
        println("\nEnter another number: ")
        //Read using Scanner class
        num2 = num_scanner.nextDouble()
        sum = getSum(num1, num2)
        println("\nSum = $sum\n")
    }
    2 -> {
        println("\nEnter a number: ")
        //Read using Scanner class
        num1 = num_scanner.nextDouble()
        println("\nEnter another number: ")
        //Read using Scanner class
        num2 = num_scanner.nextDouble()
        diff = getDifference(num1, num2)
        println("\nDifference = $diff\n")
    }
    3 -> {
        println("\nEnter a number: ")
        //Read using Scanner class
        num1 = num_scanner.nextDouble()
        println("\nEnter another number: ")
        //Read using Scanner class
        num2 = num_scanner.nextDouble()
        prod = getProduct(num1, num2)
        println("\nProduct = $prod\n")
    }
    4 -> {
        println("\nEnter a number: ")
        //Read using Scanner class
        num1 = num_scanner.nextDouble()
        println("\nEnter another number: ")
        //Read using Scanner class
        num2 = num_scanner.nextDouble()
        quo = getQuotient(num1, num2)
        println("\nQuotient = $quo\n")
```

```
        }
        5 -> {
            break
        }
        else -> {
            println("\nInvalid Choice!")
        }
    }
  }
 }
}
```

<u>Output:</u>

13.5 Oneliner functions

In a oneliner function, the body of the function comprises of an expression, result of which is returned to the calling function. General syntax:

fun <function name>(<arguments>): <optional return type> = <expression>

OR

fun <function name>(<arguments>) = <expression>

Example:

*fun tripleIt(num: Int): Int = (3 * num)*

OR

*fun tripleIt(num: Int) = (3 * num)*

In the above example, we have defined a oneliner function called **tripleIt** which triples the given integer. The above definitions are equivalent to:

fun tripleIt(num: Int): Int {
    *return (3 * num)*

}

Calling oneliner functions is the same as calling any other function. Let us write a oneliner function to multiply two numbers. We will ask the user to enter two numbers and pass them to the function:

```
/*Function Demo - Multiply two numbers*/
import java.util.Scanner
//Oneliner Function definition
```

```kotlin
fun findProduct(num1: Int, num2: Int): Int = (num1 *
num2)
    //Main function
    fun main() {
    var num1: Int
    var num2: Int
    var prod: Int
    val num_scanner = Scanner(System.`in`)
    println("\nEnter number 1: ")
    //Read using Scanner class
    num1 = num_scanner.nextInt()
    println("\nEnter number 2: ")
    //Read using Scanner class
    num2 = num_scanner.nextInt()
    prod = findProduct(num1, num2)
    println("\n$num1 x $num2 = $prod \n")
    }
```

Output:

13.6 Function overloading

A function is identified and called using its name. If all the functions in your program have a unique name, the all can be addressed uniquely. However, it is also possible to have different functions with the same name. The ambiguity in such a case is resolved based on the function parameters.

Let us say there are three functions having the same name *functionX*. First definition of *functionX* accepts <u>one integer</u>, the second definition accepts <u>an integer and a float</u> while the third definition accepts <u>one string</u>. This is how the ambiguity will be resolved – When only one integer is passed to *functionX*, the first definition of the function will be called. When an integer and a float are passed, the second definition of the function will be called. When only one string is passed, the third definition of the function is called.

Let us write two functions called *area* to calculate the areas of a triangle and rectangle. From the main function, we will call each of these definitions using suitable data types:

```
/*Function Overloading*/
import java.util.Scanner
/*Overloaded Function area:
Calculates the area of a triangle
argument 1 - base -- type Double
argument 2 - height -- type Double
return type - Double */
fun area(base: Double, height: Double): Double {
  return (base * height / 2)
}
/*Overloaded Function area:
Calculates the area of a rectangle
argument 1 - length -- type Int
argument 2 - breadth -- type Int
return type - Int */
fun area(length: Int, breadth: Int): Int {
  return (length * breadth)
}
fun main() {
  var triangle_base: Double = 20.5
```

```kotlin
    var triangle_height: Double = 30.75
    var triangle_area: Double
    var rectangle_length: Int = 10
    var rectangle_breadth: Int = 20
    var rectangle_area: Int
    //call area to calculate the area of a triangle
    triangle_area = area(triangle_base, triangle_height)
    //call area to calculate the area of a rectangle
    rectangle_area        =        area(rectangle_length,
rectangle_breadth)
    //print everything
    println("\ntriangle_base                            =
$triangle_base\ntriangle_height                          =
$triangle_height\ntriangle_area = $triangle_area")
    println("\nrectangle_length                         =
$rectangle_length\nrectangle_breadth                    =
$rectangle_breadth\nrectangle_area = $rectangle_area\n")
    }
```

Output:

13.7 Default Arguments

When a function is defined to accept arguments, we need to pass the exact number of arguments in the defined order during a function call. If the number of arguments specified in the function definition do not match the number of arguments passed at the time of the function call, there will be an error. If the correct order is not followed, the program will not work correctly or return an error. Default arguments is a feature which allows you to set default values of arguments. In case that particular argument is not passed at the time of the function call, it will not result in an error; instead, the default value will be assumed for that parameter. In order to make an argument a default one, you need to set its default value using the equal to sign. Consider the following function definition example:

fun demoFunction(x: Int, y: Int, z: Int = 0) {
*   println("$x $y $z")*
}

There is a function called **demoFunction** which accepts 3 arguments of integer type – **x, y and z**. The argument **z** is a default one having a default value of *0*. When calling this function, it will work if you pass just two arguments – **x** and **y; z's** value will be assumed to be *0*. If you pass 3 arguments, **z's** default value of 0 will be overridden with the new vale and it will work like a normal function. Let us understand this concept with an example:

```
/*Function Demo - Default Arguments*/
//Function definition
fun defArgFunction(msg: String = "Hello", num: Int =
0) {
    //Function body
    println("\nInside defArgFunction\n")
    println("\nmsg = $msg \nnum = $num\n")
}
//Main function
```

```kotlin
fun main() {
    println("\nInside    main    function.    Now    calling
defArgFunction with 2 arguments.")

    //Call defArgFunction
    defArgFunction("If    you    see    this,    it    is    not    a
default argument.", 9999)

    println("\nInside    main    function.    Now    calling
defArgFunction with 1 argument.")

    //Call defArgFunction
    defArgFunction("This is not a default argument, the
other one is!")

    println("\nInside    main    function.    Now    calling
defArgFunction with no arguments.")

    //Call defArgFunction
    defArgFunction()

    println("\nInside    main    function.    Reached    end    of
program.\n")
}
```

Output:

Note:

- A default argument should be placed at the end of the argument list. If more than one arguments will be set as default arguments, the need to be placed consecutively at the end of the argument list.

- Placing default arguments at the beginning of the argument list or somewhere in between will result in an error.

14. Arrays

An array is a collection of elements of the same data type. You can have an array of integers, floats, strings, etc. It is also possible to have an array of custom data type – for example, an array of objects. An important thing to remember here is that an array cannot contain elements of mixed type. There are many ways to declare an array, we will take a look at the simplest one using *arrayOf* function. Here is how you would declare an array:

var {array variable} = arrayOf<{optional data type}> ({element 1}, {element 2}, ... {element n})

Examples:

//Integer array of 3 elements
var numArray = arrayOf<Int> (0, 1, 2)
//String array of 4 elements
var city = arrayOf ("Denver", "Phoenix", "Chicago", "Tampa")

An array variable can be declared just like any other variable using the keywords *var* or *val*. Elements inside an array placed at array locations called indexes. An index starts at 0 and ends at one less than the size of the array. For example, if an array has a size of 10, the index will begin at 0 and end at 9. The first element of the array will be placed at index 0, the second at index 1, the third at index 2, and so on. The last element will be placed at index 9. Consider the string array from the previous code snippet:

var city = arrayOf ("Denver", "Phoenix", "Chicago", "Tampa")

Inside the city array, *"Denver"* will be placed at *index 0*, *"Phoenix"* will be placed at *index 1*, *"Chicago"* will be placed at *index 2* and *"Tampa"* will be placed at *index 3*. Here is how the array would look like inside the memory:

Array: city

Data ==>	"Denver"	"Phoenix"	"Chicago"	"Tampa"
Index ==>	0	1	2	3

When an array is declared using the arrayOf function, it also gets initialized with the list of elements supplied. From there on, the contents of the array can be changed if desired (provided the array variable is declared using the **var** keyword) but the size remains fixed. The contents of an array can be accessed using the access operator ([<index>]). For example:

var str = city[0]

The above code snippet will the first element of the array *city* and assign it to the variable *str*. Let us write a program where we will declare a few arrays and display their contents element by element:

```kotlin
/*Array Demo 1*/
fun main() {
 //Declare integer array without specifying the type
 var arr1 = arrayOf (1, 2, 3, 4, 5)
 //Declare integer array, specify type explicitly
 var arr2 = arrayOf<Int> (9, 0, 4)
 //Declare Double array, specify type explicitly
 var arr3 = arrayOf<Double> (6.8, 1.4, -5.5, 7.2)
```

```
//Declare String array, specify type explicitly
var arr4 = arrayOf<String> ("Hello", "World")
//Print Everything
println("\narr1:\n")
println("\nIndex 0 -> " + arr1[0] + "\nIndex 1 -> "
+ arr1[1] + "\nIndex 2 -> " + arr1[2] + "\nIndex 3 -> "
+ arr1[3] + "\nIndex 4 -> " + arr1[4])
println("\narr2:\n")
println("\nIndex 0 -> " + arr2[0] + "\nIndex 1 -> "
+ arr2[1] + "\nIndex 2 -> " + arr2[2])
println("\narr3:\n")
println("\nIndex 0 -> " + arr3[0] + "\nIndex 1 -> "
+ arr3[1] + "\nIndex 2 -> " + arr3[2] + "\nIndex 3 -> "
+ arr3[3])
println("\narr4:\n")
println("\nIndex 0 -> " + arr4[0] + "\nIndex 1 -> "
+ arr4[1])
   }
```

Output:

Array elements can also be fetched using the **_get_** function as follows:

<variable> = *<array variable>.get(<index>)*

Example:

str = city.get(2)

Let us write a Kotlin program to demonstrate the usage of the **_get_** function:

```kotlin
/*Array Demo 2*/
fun main() {
//Declare Double array without specifying the type
var arr1 = arrayOf (-68.6, 0, 97.1)
//Declare integer array, specify type explicitly
var arr2 = arrayOf<Int> (12, -61, 33, 21)
//Declare Double array, specify type explicitly
var arr3 = arrayOf<Double> (6.8, 1.4, -5.5, 7.2)
//Declare String array, specify type explicitly
var arr4 = arrayOf<String> ("This", "is", "Kotlin")
//Print Everything
println("\narr1:\n")
println("\nIndex 0 -> " + arr1.get(0) + "\nIndex 1
-> " + arr1.get(1) + "\nIndex 2 -> " + arr1.get(2))
println("\narr2:\n")
println("\nIndex 0 -> " + arr2.get(0) + "\nIndex 1
-> " + arr2.get(1) + "\nIndex 2 -> " + arr2.get(2) +
"\nIndex 3 -> " + arr2.get(3))
println("\narr3:\n")
println("\nIndex 0 -> " + arr3.get(0) + "\nIndex 1
-> " + arr3.get(1) + "\nIndex 2 -> " + arr3.get(2) +
"\nIndex 3 -> " + arr3.get(3))
println("\narr4:\n")
println("\nIndex 0 -> " + arr4.get(0) + "\nIndex 1
-> " + arr4.get(1) + "\nIndex 2 -> " + arr4.get(2))
}
```

Output:

In both the previous examples, we have accessed array elements manually by addressing each array index one by one. Using a loop can automate this process. There are no hard and fast rules when it comes to using loops with arrays. Having said that, using a loop variable to traverse through array index is a common programming practice. Here is a programming example:

```kotlin
/*Array Demo 3*/
fun main() {
  //Declare integer array without specifying the type
  var arr = arrayOf (18, 36, 20, -61, 40, 38)
  //Declare and initialize a loop variable
  var i: Int = 0
  println("\narr:\n")
  //Loop from 0 to 5
  while (i < 6) {
      //print arr[i]
```

```
println("\nIndex $i -> " + arr[i])
//Increment i to move to the next index
i++
    }
}
```

Output:

```
F:\Kotlin\Programs>kotlinc array3.kt -include-runtime -d array3.jar
F:\Kotlin\Programs>java -jar array3.jar
arr:

Index 0 -> 18
Index 1 -> 36
Index 2 -> 20
Index 3 -> -61
Index 4 -> 40
Index 5 -> 38
F:\Kotlin\Programs>_
```

Apart from using the access operator to access the elements, *get* function can be used to do the same. Here is the general syntax:

<variable> = <array variable>.get(<index>)

Example:

x = num_array.get(3)

In the above code snippet, the third element from the array **num_array** will be fetched and assigned to **x**. Let us see this function in action:

```
/*Array Demo 4*/
fun main() {
//Declare string array without specifying the type
    var name_array = arrayOf ("Susan", "Jared",
"Dillon", "Caleb", "Lilly")
    //Declare and initialize a loop variable
    var i: Int = 0
    println("\nname_arr:\n")
    //Loop from 0 to 4
    while (i < 5) {
        //print name_array[i]
        println("\nIndex $i -> " + name_array.get(i))
        //Increment i to move to the next index
        i++
    }
}
```

Output:

14.1 Array modification

Just as array elements can be accessed by specifying the index with the help of the access operator, the same method can be used in a reverse order to set/modify values at a given index location. It is important to note that only existing elements can be modified. No new elements can be added as the size of the array remains fixed. Here is the general syntax:

<array variable>[<index>] = <variable/constant/expression>

Example:

name[9] = "Peter"

Let us write a Kotlin program to initialize an array first, then modify its contents and print the back:

```
/*Array Demo 5*/
fun main() {
 //Declare integer array without specifying the type
 var arr = arrayOf (-43, 0, 16, 33, -72, 47)
 //Declare and initialize a loop variable
 var i: Int = 0
 println("\narr (original):\n")
 //Loop from 0 to 5
 while (i < 6) {
     //print arr[i]
     println("\nIndex $i -> " + arr[i])
     //Increment i to move to the next index
     i++
 }
 //Making changes to arr
 arr[0] = 25
 arr[1] = 31
 arr[2] = 0
 arr[3] = -67
 arr[4] = -99
 arr[5] = 21
 //Set loop variable i to 0
 i = 0
 //Reprint arr
 println("\narr (after modification):\n")
```

```kotlin
//Loop from 0 to 5
while (i < 6) {
    //print arr[i]
    println("\nIndex $i -> " + arr[i])
    //Increment i to move to the next index
    i++
}
}
```

Output:

Let us take another programming example where we will create an array of five empty strings, ask the user to input 5 strings one by one. We will then add these strings to the appropriate locations in the array and finally print the whole array:

```kotlin
/*Array Demo 6*/
fun main() {
    //Declare string array of empty strings
    var strArray = arrayOf<String> ("", "", "", "", "")
```

```kotlin
//Declare and initialize a loop variable
var i: Int = 0
//Declare string variable to store input
var strInput: String
//Loop from 0 to 4
while (i < 5) {
    //Prompt the user to enter a string
    println("\nEnter the string to be placed at
Index $i: ")
    //Read user input using readLine
    strInput = readLine()!!
    //Assign input to the array at an appropriate
index
    strArray[i] = strInput
    //Increment i to move to the next index
    i++
}
i = 0
//Loop from 0 to 4
while (i < 5) {
    //print strArray elements, fetch using got
function
    println("\nIndex $i -> " + strArray.get(i))
    //Increment i to move to the next index
    i++
}
}
```

Output:

Apart from using the access operator to modify element values, you can use the *set* function as follows:

<array variable>.set(<index>, <value>)

Example:

city_array.set(2, "Tokyo")

Let us see how set function works with the help of a programming example:

```
/*Array Demo 7*/
import java.util.Scanner
fun main() {
 //Declare int array
 var numArray = arrayOf (0, 0, 0, 0)
 //Declare and initilize a loop variable
 var i: Int = 0
 //Declare a variable to store user input
 var num: Int
```

```kotlin
    val num_scanner = Scanner(System.`in`)
    //Loop from 0 to 3
    while (i < 4) {
        //Prompt the user to enter a string
        println("\nEnter the number to be placed at
Index $i: ")
        //Read user input using scanner object
        num = num_scanner.nextInt()
        //Assign input to the array at an appropriate
index using set function
        numArray.set(i, num)
        //Increment i to move to the next index
        i++
    }
    i = 0
    //Loop from 0 to 4
    while (i < 4) {
        //print numArray[i]
        println("\nIndex $i -> " + numArray[i])
        //Increment i to move to the next index
        i++
    }
}
```

Output:

14.2 for Loop and Arrays

In the *Loops* section under the *Control Flow* chapter, we had only covered *while loop* and *do while loop*. The *for loop* was kept out on purpose. This was because, in order to understand how a for loop works, you need to understand how collections work. Array is a type of collection and now that we have learnt how arrays work, we can take a look at how for loop works. Here is the general syntax:

for (<element variable> in <array variable>) {
//Statements
}

A for loop can be used to iterate through an array, marked by **<array variable>** in the above code snippet. During the first iteration of the loop, the first element of the array will be fetched into the specified variable, marked by **<element variable>**. During the second iteration, the second element will be fetched and so on. This process will happen automatically till the last element of the array is fetched. We can say that the number of iterations that a for loop will go through will be equal to the number of elements of the given array provided there is no use of loop control statements like **break** and **continue**. Let us write a program to use for loops to iterate through multiple arrays:

```
/*Array Demo 8*/
fun main() {
 //Declare integer array
 var intArray = arrayOf (165, -325, 617)
 //Declare Double array, specify type explicitly
 var doubleArray = arrayOf<Double> (9.23, -3.25,
6.02, 0.75, 9.64, -1.01, 8.53)
```

```
    //Declare String array, specify type explicitly
    var strArray = arrayOf<String> ("Laptop", "book",
"World", "Airport", "Smartphone", "Travel", "Apps")
    //Print Everything
    println("\nintArray:\n")
    for (num in intArray) {
        println(num)
    }
    println("\ndoubleArray:\n")
    for (x in doubleArray) {
        println(x)
    }
    println("\nstrArray:\n")
    for (word in strArray) {
        println(word)
    }
}
```

Output:

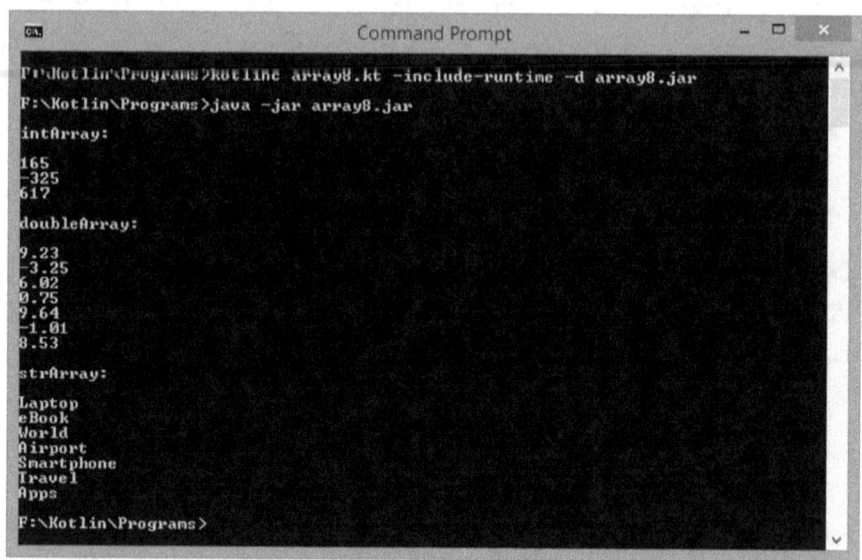

Note: Do not try to refer to an array index that does not exist. This will return an array out of bounds error.

15. Strings

A string is a sequence of characters. We have used strings throughout this book in programming examples and otherwise. In this section, we will learn a few more useful things about strings. Let us recap what we already know. This is how we used to declare and initialize strings:

var <string variable>: String = "<sequence of characters>"

Example:

var word: String = "Alpha"

A string enclosed within double quotes is known as an **escaped string**. You can make use of escape character sequence inside an escaped string and it will have a particular meaning. For example, if you use *"\t"* inside an escaped string, it will leave a tab-space indent. There is another kind of a string called a **raw string** which is enclosed between three double quotes. Such a string can span over multiple lines, using escape characters inside this string will have no meaning, they will be printed as they are. Here is an example of a raw string:

var s: String = """

This is the first line of the string.

This is the second line.

"""

Note: Leading white-spaces from a string can be removed using a function called **trimMargin()**. If **str** is the string, **str.trimMargin()**

will remove all the leading white-spaces and return a new string. This function can work on escaped as well as raw strings.

The size of the string can be determined using the **_length_** property of the **_String class_**. This is how to use it:

<variable> = <string variable>.length

Example:

var msg: String = "Great book"
val len = msg.length

Let us write a program and demonstrate the string concepts that we learned so far:

```kotlin
/*Strings demo 1*/
fun main() {
 //Declare some strings
 val str1 = "This is an escaped string."
 val str2 = """This is a raw string."""
 val str3 = """
A raw string
enclosed within 3 double quotes
can span over multiple lines.
"""
 val str4 = str3.trimMargin()
 //Fetch string size
 val len_str1 = str1.length
 val len_str2 = str2.length
 val len_str3 = str3.length
 val len_str4 = str4.length
 //Print everything
 println("\nstr1: $str1 | Length: $len_str1\n")
 println("\nstr2: $str2 | Length: $len_str2\n")
 println("\nstr3: $str3 | Length: $len_str3\n")
 println("\nstr4: $str4 | Length: $len_str4\n")
}
```

Output:

```
C:\Windows\system32\cmd.exe

F:\Kotlin\Programs>kotlinc strdemo1.kt -include-runtime -d strdemo1.jar
F:\Kotlin\Programs>java -jar strdemo1.jar
str1: This is an escaped string. | Length: 26

str2: This is a raw string. | Length: 21

str3:
        A raw string
        enclosed within 3 double quotes
        can span over multiple lines.
        | Length: 81

str4:   A raw string
        enclosed within 3 double quotes
        can span over multiple lines. | Length: 78

F:\Kotlin\Programs>_
```

Individual characters of a string can be accessed by specifying index inside the access operator ([]). Similar to arrays, string indexes range from 0 till one less than the string size. However, strings are *immutable*. That is, individual characters can only be read but not modified. If the string has been declared with the *var* keyword, a new string value can be assigned to it as a whole but again, individual characters cannot be modified. Here is a program that reads characters of a string one by one:

```kotlin
/*Strings demo 2*/
fun main() {
 var str = "Simple String"
 val len = str.length
 println("\nstr: $str | Length: $len\n")
 //Print character by character
 println("\nIndex 0: " + str[0])
 println("Index 1: " + str[1])
 println("Index 2: " + str[2])
 println("Index 3: " + str[3])
 println("Index 4: " + str[4])
```

```
    println("Index 5: " + str[5])
    println("Index 6: " + str[6])
    println("Index 7: " + str[7])
    println("Index 8: " + str[8])
    println("Index 9: " + str[9])
    println("Index 10: " + str[10])
    println("Index 11: " + str[11])
    println("Index 12: " + str[12])
}
```

Output:

You can also use loops to simplify this process:

```
/*Strings demo 3*/
fun main() {
 var str = "Hello from Kotlin!"
 val len = str.length
 var i: Int = 0
 println("\nstr: $str | Length: $len\n\n")
 while (i < len) {
     println("Index $i -> " + str[i])
     i++
 }
}
```

Output:

```
C:\Windows\system32\cmd.exe                          _  □  ×

F:\Kotlin\Programs>java -jar strdemo3.jar

str: Hello from Kotlin! | Length: 18

Index 0 -> H
Index 1 -> e
Index 2 -> l
Index 3 -> l
Index 4 -> o
Index 5 ->
Index 6 -> f
Index 7 -> r
Index 8 -> o
Index 9 -> m
Index 10 ->
Index 11 -> K
Index 12 -> o
Index 13 -> t
Index 14 -> l
Index 15 -> i
Index 16 -> n
Index 17 -> !

F:\Kotlin\Programs>_
```

An array of characters can be converted to a string and a string can be converted to an array of characters using *String constructor* and *toCharArray function* respectively. Here is how to do it:

// Declare a character array:

var chArray1 = charArrayOf ('H', 'e', 'l', 'l', 'o', ' ', 'W', 'o', 'r', 'l', 'd', '!')

// Convert to string using String constructor

var str = String(chArray1)

// Convert a string to character array

var chArray2 = str.toCharArray()

These two methods can be particularly useful if you want to modify individual characters of a string. Since this cannot be done directly, there is a workaround – first, the target string will have to be converted to an array of characters using the toCharArray function. Next, modifications can be done to the individual elements of this array. Finally, the modified array can be converted back to a string. Here is a Kotlin program that does exactly this:

```kotlin
/*Strings demo 4*/
fun main() {
val chArray1 = charArrayOf ('e', 'B', 'o', 'o', 'k')
 val str1 = String(chArray1)
 var str2: String = "Mike"
 var chArray2 = str2.toCharArray()
 println("\nchArray1:\n")
 var i: Int = 0
 while (i < chArray1.size) {
    println("Index $i -> " + chArray1[i])
    i++
 }
 println("\n\nString formed using chArray1 -> str1:
$str1")
 println("\n\nstr2: $str2")
 println("\n\nCharacter array formed using str2: \n")
 println("\nchArray2:\n")
 i = 0
 while (i < chArray2.size) {
    println("Index $i -> " + chArray2[i])
    i++
 }
 //Change values at index 0 and 1 in chArray2
 chArray2[0] = 'B'
 chArray2[1] = 'a'
 //Form a new string with modified chArray2
 val str3 = String(chArray2)
 println("\n\nstr3 formed by modifying chArray2:
$str3\n")
 }
```

Output:

```
C:\Windows\system32\cmd.exe                              -  □  ×
F:\Kotlin\Programs>kotlinc strdemo4.kt -include-runtime -d strdemo4.jar

F:\Kotlin\Programs>java -jar strdemo4.jar

chArray1:

Index 0 -> e
Index 1 -> B
Index 2 -> o
Index 3 -> o
Index 4 -> k

String formed using chArray1 -> str1: eBook

str2: Mike

Character array formed using str2:

chArray2:

Index 0 -> M
Index 1 -> i
Index 2 -> k
Index 3 -> e

str3 formed by modifying chArray2: Bake

F:\Kotlin\Programs>
```

15.1 String Concatenation

Two or more strings can be concatenated using *string interpolation* or by using the ***plus operator (+)***. String interpolation is where the dollar sign is prefixed to a variable name inside a string. We have done this several times to print values of variables in many programs. Here is an example of string interpolation:

var s1 = "Good"

var s2 = "Morning"

var s3 = "$s1 $s2"

When using string interpolation, the value of the variable prefixed with dollar sign will be substituted where the said variable is placed.

Using plus sign to concatenate strings is also easy. Here is the general syntax:

\<string variable\> = \<string 1\> + \<string 2\> + ... + \<string n\>

Example:

s = s1 + s2 + ... + sn

Let us write a Kotlin program to demonstrate string concatenation:

```
/*String Concatenation*/
fun main() {
 var firstName = "Rupa"
 var lastName = "Jayasurya"
 var city = "Colombo"
 var country = "Sri Lanka"
 var name = "$firstName $lastName"
 var address = city + ", " + country
 println("\nFirst    Name:    $firstName\nLast    Name:
$lastName\nFull Name: $name")
    println("\nCity: $city\nCountry: $country\nAddress:
$address\n")
    }
```

Output:

```
F:\Kotlin\Programs>kotlinc strdemo5.kt -include-runtime -d strdemo5.jar

F:\Kotlin\Programs>java -jar strdemo5.jar

First Name: Rupa
Last Name: Jayasurya
Full Name: Rupa Jayasurya

City: Colombo
Country: Sri Lanka
Address: Colombo, Sri Lanka

F:\Kotlin\Programs>
```

15.2 Substring

Getting a substring from another string can be done using the *substring* function as follows:

<substring variable> = <string variable>.substring(<start index>, <end index>)

Example:

s1 = s2.substring(5, 9)

Here is a programming example:

```
/*Strings demo 6*/
fun main() {
  var str1 = "Google put a lot of weight behing
Kotlin language!"
  val str2 = str1.substring(0, 26)
  println("\nstr1 = $str1 \nstr2 = $str2\n")
}
```

<u>Output:</u>

15.3 Check for the presence of a substring

The *contains* function can be used to check for the presence of a string within another string. This function returns *true* if the given string is present and *false* if not present. Here is the general syntax:

```
if (<string 1>.contains(<string 2>)) {
    //Code to be executed if the string is present
}
else {
    //Code to be executed if the string is present
}
```

Note: An optional parameter called **ignoreCase** can be set to **true** (it is **false** by default) while passing **<string 2>** to the **contains** function. While searching for the string, case sensitivity will be ignored. Here is how to do it – *<string 1>.contains(<string 2>, ignoreCase = true).*

Let us write a program where in we will ask the user to enter two strings and check if the second string is present in the first string:

```
/*Strings demo 7*/
fun main() {
 println("\nEnter a string: ")
 val str1 = readLine()!!
 println("\nEnter the string to be searched: ")
 val str2 = readLine()!!
 if (str1.contains(str2)) {
     println("\n$str2 is present in $str1")
 }
 else {
     println("\n$str2 is NOT present in $str1")
 }
}
```

Output:

15.4 String search

A string can be searched within another string using the *indexOf* function. The function returns the first occurrence of the given substring. If it is not found, *-1* is returned. General syntax:

<location variable> = <string 1>.indexOf(<string 2>)

Example:

var loc = s1.indexOf(s2)

Note: An optional parameter called ***ignoreCase*** can be set to **true** (it is **false** by default) while passing **<string 2>** to the **indexOf** function. The case of both strings will not be considered if this parameter is set to true. Here is how to do it — *<string 1>.indexOf(<string 2>, ignoreCase = true).*

Let us write a program where in we will ask the user to enter two strings and check if the second string is present in the first string and if so, find its location:

```kotlin
/*Strings demo 8*/
fun main() {
 println("\nEnter a string: ")
 val str1 = readLine()!!
 println("\nEnter the string to be searched: ")
 val str2 = readLine()!!
 if (str1.contains(str2)) {
     val loc = str1.indexOf(str2)
     println("\n$str2 found at index $loc in $str1")
 }
 else {
     println("\n$str2 is NOT present in $str1")
 }
}
```

Output:

```
F:\Kotlin\Programs>kotlinc strdemo8.kt -include-runtime -d strdemo8.jar
F:\Kotlin\Programs>java -jar strdemo8.jar
Enter a string:
Sunridge Way NE, Calgary, Alberta, Canada
Enter the string to be searched:
Calgary
Calgary found at index 17 in Sunridge Way NE, Calgary, Alberta, Canada
F:\Kotlin\Programs>java -jar strdemo8.jar
Enter a string:
Oxford St, Marylebone, London, UK
Enter the string to be searched:
Street
Street is NOT present in Oxford St, Marylebone, London, UK
F:\Kotlin\Programs>
```

15.5 String comparison

Two strings can be compared for equality using **== operator** or by using the **equals** function. Both the methods will return **true** if the given strings are equal and **false** if not equal. Here is how to compare two strings:

```
//Using == operator
if (<string 1> == <string 2>) {
    //Both strings are the same
    //Do something when they are the same
}
else {
    //Both strings are not the same
    //Do something else when they are not the same
}
//Using equals functional
if (<string 1>.equals(<string 2>)) {
    //Both strings are the same
    //Do something when they are the same
}
else {
    //Both strings are not the same
    //Do something else when they are not the same
}
```

Here is a Kotlin program that demonstrates string comparison:

```
/*Strings demo 9*/
fun main() {
 println("\nEnter a string: ")
```

```kotlin
val str1 = readLine()!!
println("\nEnter another string: ")
val str2 = readLine()!!
if (str1.equals(str2)) {
    println("\nBoth strings are the same.")
}
else {
    println("\nBoth strings are NOT the same.")
}
}
```

Output:

16. Command Line Arguments

Command line argument is an argument passed to an application via the command line. Command line arguments are specified after the name of the application and are separated by spaces. There are many benefits of using command line arguments. Once of the most significant one is that these arguments can serve as input to the application. The main function should be written in a way that it is ready to accept arguments. Here is how you would slightly modify the main function:

fun main (args: Array<string>) {
    //Statements

}

The parameter **args** is an array of strings where the command line arguments will be stored. An important property of the Array class called **size** can be used to determine the number of elements in an array. In this case, the size of args array will tell us the number of arguments the user has passed. General syntax:

num = args.size

When a user specifies command line arguments, they will be stored in the args array in the order that they are passed. That is, the first argument will be stored at index 0, the second one at index 1 and so on.

Now that we know where command line arguments will be stored and how to access them, let us see how they are passed to an application – in order to specify command line arguments for an application, use the following syntax:

java -jar <kotlinApplication.jar> <argument 1> <argument 2>, ... , <argument n>

Example:

java -jar myProgram.jar hello world 1 2 3

Note: The compilation process remains the same whether or not you plan to pass command line arguments. Only the execution process includes one extra step of passing arguments.

In the above example, we are executing **myProgram.jar** application and passing 5 arguments to it – **hello, world, 1, 2** and **3**. If the code of this application is written to accept arguments, **hello** will be stored at **args[0]**, **world** at **args[1]**, **1** at **args[2]**, **2** at **args[3]** and **3** at **args[4]**.

Note:

1. args is an array of String. Even if you pass numbers, they will be treated as strings. If you want to pass numbers for performing mathematical operations, the arguments in string format need to be converted to the appropriate numerical format first.

2. If you want a string having spaces to be considered as one argument, the string should be enclosed within double quotes.

Let us write a simple program to determine the number of arguments passed.

```
/*Command line arguments*/
fun main (args: Array<String>) {
 println("Number of arguments: " + args.size)
}
```

Output:

Let us modify this program to print all the arguments:

```
/*Command line arguments*/
fun main (args: Array<String>) {
 println("\nNumber of arguments: " + args.size)
 if (args.size > 0) {
     println("\nCommand line arguments: \n")
     var i: Int = 0
     while (i < args.size) {
     //Print args[i]
     println("\nIndex $i -> " + args[i])
     //Increment i to move to the next index
     i++
     }
 }
}
```

Output:

```
F:\Kotlin\Programs>kotlinc -include-runtime cla2.kt -d cla2.jar
F:\Kotlin\Programs>java -jar cla2.jar Hello World "Kotlin is a great programming
 language" 4 -2 0 Bye
Number of arguments: 7
Command line arguments:

Index 0 -> Hello
Index 1 -> World
Index 2 -> Kotlin is a great programming language
Index 3 -> 4
Index 4 -> -2
Index 5 -> 0
Index 6 -> Bye
F:\Kotlin\Programs>
```

Let us write a program to add all the numbers passed as command line arguments and print the sum. As mentioned earlier, all the arguments will be treated as string and hence conversion to the appropriate data type will be needed. Here, we will convert string equivalent numbers to Double type:

```kotlin
/*Command line arguments*/
fun main (args: Array<String>) {
  if (args.size > 0) {
      var i: Int = 0
      var sum: Double = 0.0
      while (i < args.size) {
          val num = args[i].toDouble()
          sum = sum + num
          i++
      }
      println("\nSum = $sum\n")
  }
  else {
      println("\nKindly pass numbers as command line
arguments.\n")
```

```
    }
  }
```

Output:

Let us write another program where we will pass two strings are command line arguments and check if they are equal:

```kotlin
/*Command line arguments - str comp*/
fun main (args: Array<String>) {
  if (args.size == 2) {
      val str1 = args[0]
      val str2 = args[1]
      if (str1.equals(str2)) {
          println("\nBoth strings are the same.")
      }
      else {
          println("\nBoth strings are NOT the same.")
      }
  }
  else {
      println("\nKindly pass two strings as command
line arguments.\n")
  }
}
```

Output:

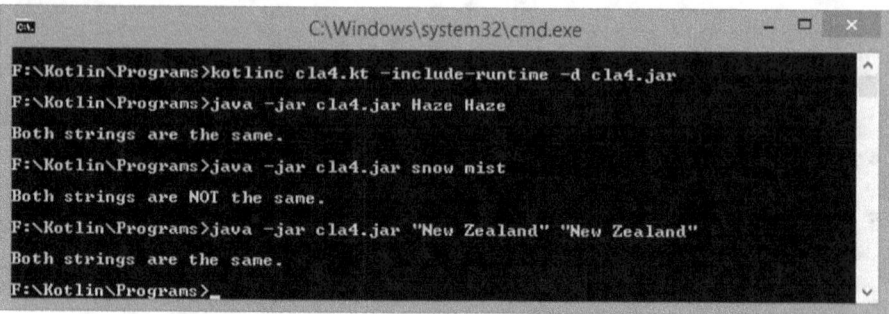

```
F:\Kotlin\Programs>kotlinc cla4.kt -include-runtime -d cla4.jar
F:\Kotlin\Programs>java -jar cla4.jar Haze Haze
Both strings are the same.
F:\Kotlin\Programs>java -jar cla4.jar snow mist
Both strings are NOT the same.
F:\Kotlin\Programs>java -jar cla4.jar "New Zealand" "New Zealand"
Both strings are the same.
F:\Kotlin\Programs>_
```

17. Introduction to Classes and Objects

Kotlin is an Object Oriented Programming (OOP) language. A lot of chapters before this one made use of OOP concepts and hence a chapter on introduction to OOP was placed in the first half of this book (**Chapter 9**). That chapter was largely theoretical, just talked about what are classes and objects and their significance. In this chapter, we will learn to create our own classes and objects. We will be using an IDE (IntelliJ IDAE or Eclipse) as there is going to be a configuration overhead should you try to build code that has class declaration using the command line compiler. Also, most of the production level Kotlin development that is happening today uses OOP concepts extensively and is done using IDEs.

A class is a definition of a user defined data type. It can contain variables called data members and functions called member functions which are responsible for accessing the data members. An object is an instance of a class which has its own copies of data members.

Here is the general syntax to declare a class:

class <Class Name> {
    //Data members
    //Member functional
}

Example:

class Car {
    val make: String = ""

```
        val model: String = ""
        val cc: Int = 0
        val cost: Double = 0.0

}
```

Note: Class declaration should be done outside all functions.

The Car class shown in the above code snippet has 4 data members of different data types. ***Data members need to be initialized when declared***. An object of a class can be created using the following syntax:

val <object name> = <class name>()

Example:

```
val c1 = Car()
var c2 = Car()
```

Data members of objects can be accessed (read/write) using the dot operator as follows:

//Write

<object name>.<data member> = <value>

Example:

```
c1.make = "Jaguar"
//Read
<variable> = <object>.<data member>
car_name = c2.model
```

Let us create a class **called Person** with data member – **name, age, gender** and **country**. We will create two objects of class Person – ***p1*** and ***p2***, set their properties and display them:

```kotlin
class Person {
//Declare Data Members/Properties and Initialize
var name: String = ""
var age: Int = 0
//Initialize gender to a null value, could use any
other arbitrary value
var gender: Char = '\u0000'
var country: String = ""
}
fun main () {
//Create an object of class Person - p1
val p1 = Person()
//Set properties of p1
p1.name = "Pedro Fernandez"
p1.age = 41
p1.gender = 'M'
p1.country = "Argentina"
//Create an object of class Person - p2
val p2 = Person()
//Set properties of p2
p2.name = "Victoria Lewandowski"
p2.age = 34
p2.gender = 'F'
p2.country = "Russia"
//Print everything
println("\nObject p1:\nName: " + p1.name + "\nAge:
" + p1.age + "\nGender: " + p1.gender + "\nCountry: " +
p1.country)
println("\nObject p2:\nName: " + p2.name + "\nAge:
" + p2.age + "\nGender: " + p2.gender + "\nCountry: " +
p2.country)
}
```

Output (IntelliJ IDEA):

```
Run:      Oop1Kt

    "C:\Program Files\Java\jdk-11.0.8\bin\java.exe" "-javaagent:

    Object p1:
    Name: Pedro Fernandez
    Age: 41
    Gender: M
    Country: Argentina

    Object p2:
    Name: Victoria Lewandowski
    Age: 34
    Gender: F
    Country: Russia

    Process finished with exit code 0
```

There is something called as *visibility modifier* in Kotlin. A visibility modifier will define how a particular data member or a member function can be accessed. There are four visibility modifiers in Kotlin – *private, protected, internal* and *public*. *When no visibility modifier is specified, it is considered as public.* A public data member or member function can be accessed from anywhere, even from outside the class. In the above example, all the data members were defined as public (considered as public as no modifier was specified). That is the reason why we were able to access them from outside the class – i.e main function. A private data member cannot be accessed from outside the class and is only visible to the member functions of that particular class. Declaring data members as private and member functions as public is a simple and good object oriented programming practice. Internal and protected visibility modifiers require advanced OOP knowledge and hence will not be covered. In order to set visibility of a data member, the visibility modifier should be placed before the val/var keyword. Consider the following code snippet:

```
class Smartphone {
    private val make: String = ""
    private val model: String =""
}
```

Smartphone class has two data members of type string – **make** and **model**. Both these data members are declared as **private** and hence will not be accessible from outside the class. Only member functions of Smartphone class can access these data members.

17.1 Member functions

A member function of a class is used to access data members of the same class. Since it is declared inside the class, all data members and other member functions can be accessed from the said member function. The syntax of defining a member function is the same as defining any other function. Consider the following code snippet:

```
//Class declaration
class ABC {
    //Data Member
    private x: Int = 0
    //Member Functions
    //Set data
```

```kotlin
    fun setX(num: Int) {
        x = num
    }
    //Print data
    fun showX() {
        println("x: $x")
    }
}
//Main function
fun main() {
    //Create an object of ABC class
    val obj1 = ABC()
    //Call setX to set value of x
    obj1.setX(6)
    //Call showX to print the value of X
    obj1.showX()
}
```

In the above program, there is a class called ABC, inside it there is a private data member called **x** of **Int** type. Since this is a private data member, it cannot be accessed directly from the main function. There are two functions – **setX** and **showX** to solve this problem. The function **setX** accepts one argument and assigns it to **x** data member while the **showX** functions prints the value of **x.** Both member functions are public. Inside the main function, we create an object of **ABC** class – **obj1.** Then we call the **setX** function using the **obj1.setX(6)** statement, **6** is passed as an argument to **setX.** Once this function is called, **obj1's x** property will be set to *6.* Finally, we print the value of *x* using the statement *obj1.showX()*.

Let us write a Kotlin program to demonstrate the usage of member functions:

```kotlin
class Employee {
//Declare    Private    Data    Members/Properties    and
Initialize
//Private variables cannot be accessed directly from
outside the class.
//Only member functions can do so.
private var empName: String = ""
private var empAge: Int = 0
private var empId: Int = 0
//Initialize gender to a null value, could use any
other arbitrary value
private var empGender: Char = '\u0000'
//Member function to set data members
fun setData(name: String, age: Int, id: Int, gender:
Char) {
//Set properties of the current object
empName = name
empAge = age
empId = id
empGender = gender
}
//Member function to print data members
fun showData () {
//Print details of the current object
println("\nName:    $empName\nID:    $empId\nAge:
$empAge\nGender: $empGender")
}
}
fun main() {
//Create objects of class Employee
```

```kotlin
val e1 = Employee()
val e2 = Employee()
//Set data members of e1 and e2 using setData member
function
e1.setData("Vir", 23, 5629, 'M')
e2.setData("Yami", 27, 3801, 'F')
//Print data using showData member function
println("\nObject e1:\n")
e1.showData()
println("\nObject e2:\n")
e2.showData()
}
```

Output (IntelliJ IDEA):

```
Run:    Oop2Kt ×

        "C:\Program Files\Java\jdk-11.0.8\bin\java.exe" "-javaagent

        Object e1:


        Name: Vir
        ID: 5629
        Age: 23
        Gender: M


        Object e2:


        Name: Yami
        ID: 3801
        Age: 27
        Gender: F


        Process finished with exit code 0
```

17.2 Constructors

A constructor is a special kind of member function that is used to initialize data members of an object at the time of object creation. A class can have one primary constructor and zero or more secondary constructors. We will be learning only about primary constructors. Let us recall the *Car class* from the beginning of this chapter:

```
class Car {
        val make: String = ""
        val model: String = ""
        val cc: Int = 0
        val cost: Double = 0.0
}
```

This is how we would create objects of Car class:

```
val c1 = Car()
```

Car() part of the above statement actually calls the constructor of Car class. Since we have not written the logic for a primary constructor, this statement will simply create an object of Car type. A simple primary constructor can be defined during class declaration itself as follows:

```
class <class name> (<data members to be initialized>) {
        //Statements
}
```

Example:

```
class Car(make: String, model: String, cc: Int, cost: Double) {
```

```
//Data members
//Member functions
}
```

An object can be initialized by directly passing the parameters at the time of object creation. For example, a Car object initialization would look like:

val c1 = Car ("Jeep", "Compass", 2000, 25000)

The above statement will create and initialize a Car object. The property **make** will be set to *"Jeep"*, **model** will be set to *"Compass"*, **cc** will be set to *2000* and **cost** will be set to *25000*. Initialization will happen automatically and no separate piece of code is needed.

Let us modify the previous programming example involving class Employee. Instead of using the **setData** function to set data members, we will use a constructor to initialize Employee objects:

```
class Employee (val empName: String, val empAge: Int,
val empId: Int, val empGender: Char) {
//Member function to print data members
fun showData () {
//Print details of the current object
println("\nName:      $empName\nID:       $empId\nAge:
$empAge\nGender: $empGender")
}
}
fun main() {
//Create objects of class Employee, send parameters
to the constructor
val e1 = Employee("Greta", 29, 9104, 'F')
val e2 = Employee("Teena", 25, 8239, 'F')
//Print data using showData member function
```

```
println("\nObject e1:\n")
e1.showData()
println("\nObject e2:\n")
e2.showData()
}
```

Output (Eclipse):

Problems @ Javadoc Declaration Console ⊠ Progress
<terminated> Config - oop3.kt [Java Application]

```
Object e1:

Name: Greta
ID: 9104
Age: 29
Gender: F

Object e2:

Name: Teena
ID: 8239
Age: 25
Gender: F
```

If you want to perform some other operations at the time of object creation, you can use the initializer block inside the class definition as follows:

class ABC {

   //Data members

   ...

   //Member functions

   ...

```
//Init Block
init {
    //Statements to be executed when an object is created
}
}
```

When an object is created, the *init* block will be invoked and statements inside it will be executed one by one.

18. Final Words

This book was written during the COVID-19 pandemic. IT professionals always knew that most of the software development that is happening inside expensive office spaces can also be done from home. The pandemic era gave an opportunity to put the work from home concept to real test. In most cases an average software developer will need a decently powered computer system and a stable internet connection in order to carry out development work. The reason behind mentioning this fact is to motivate you. Of course a lot of software development is happening using programming languages such as C/C++, Java, HTML, JS, etc. But Kotlin is picking up pace. Especially after Google announced that Kotlin is now a preferred language for Android application development.

I have tried my best to cover basic concepts of Kotlin. If you have understood these basic concepts well and want to learn more, I strongly suggest going deeper into object oriented. Web development and android application development use OOP heavily. Even if you are a hobbyist and if this book managed to spark some interest within you, there are plenty of resources on the internet with which you can learn a lot more. Some of the advanced topics include Exception Handling, File I/O, etc.

Hope you have learned something of value from my book!

If you enjoyed this book as much as I've enjoyed writing it, you can subscribe* to my email list for exclusive content and sneak peaks of my future books.

Visit the link below:

http://eepurl.com/du_L4n

OR

Use the QR Code:

(*Must be 13 years or older to subscribe)